THE *JOY* OF PERSONAL WORSHIP

LYNNE HYBELS

This book is designed for your personal reading pleasure and profit. It is also designed for group study. A leader's guide with helps and hints for teachers and visual aids (Victor Multiuse Transparency Masters) is available from your local bookstore or from the publisher.

VICTOR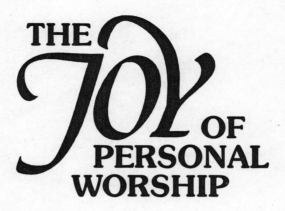

BOOKS a division of SP Publications, Inc.
WHEATON, ILLINOIS 60187

Offices also in
Whitby, Ontario, Canada
Amersham-on-the-Hill, Bucks, England

Unless otherwise noted, Scripture quotations are taken from the *New American Standard Bible,* © the Lockman Foundation, 1960, 1962, 1963, 1968, 1971, 1972, 1973, 1975, 1977. Other quotations are from *The Holy Bible: New International Version* (NIV), © 1978 by the New York International Bible Society and the *King James Version* (KJV). Used by permission.

Recommended Dewey Decimal Classification: 248.3
Suggested Subject Heading: WORSHIP

Library of Congress Catalog Card Number: 84-50140
ISBN: 0-89693-373-3

VICTOR BOOKS
A division of SP Publications, Inc.
        Wheaton, Illinois 60187

Contents

Introduction

When I signed the contract to write this book, I did so with mixed feelings. On one hand, I was incredibly excited. I couldn't believe God's grace in giving me this golden opportunity. How I appreciated the editors at Victor Books who expressed their confidence in my abilities and their interest in personal worship. I knew that working on this book would lead me on a life-changing journey that I desperately wanted to take.

On the other hand, I was nearly overwhelmed with apprehension. Did I have the necessary skills? Would I be able to find time to work on it? Would the kids adjust to the new schedule? Would it tax my relationship with Bill? Could I meet the deadline?

Jumping back and forth between my excitement and my fear, I concluded that to succeed in this project I had to commit myself to discipline, careful scheduling, and conscientious goal-setting. I firmly believed that if I applied myself with diligence, surely God would give me the strength and creativity needed.

But after one month of disciplined work, I realized that my perseverance was not paying off. I was frustrated and even more fearful than ever. Though I was studying and absorbing plenty of new information, I couldn't get a word down on paper.

"Lord," I prayed, "what's wrong? I really thought You wanted me to take on this project. I thought You were going to help me. I thought this would bring honor to You. What has happened? Why am I so empty?"

The answer was obvious. In the hectic schedule of studying and reading and learning about worship, I had become a *non*worshiper. In readjusting my schedule so that I could concentrate on the *subject* of worship, I had ignored the *object* of worship—my Lord. Worship had become something I *should* do, not something I did.

I had allowed my writing to take precedence over my God. *Oh, He will understand,* I thought. *He knows I have a deadline.* But my study was fruitless, the outline was disorganized, and the words just wouldn't come. And with my personal failure, the Lord humbled me. Graciously, He reminded me that except I abide in Him, I can do nothing (John 15:5).

This is not a book on corporate worship. Here you will read nothing about worship services or high and low liturgies. There have been many good books written on these subjects and I hope they will be widely read. God is vitally concerned about the corporate worship of His church. Undoubtedly, few things give Him greater pleasure than the gathering together of believers in worship.

So why have I neglected the subject of corporate worship? Because I firmly believe that *corporate* worship will only be meaningful and pleasing to God if it is a natural outgrowth of *personal* worship, which begins in the quietness of our own hearts.

Worship is a discipline. Though God intended worship to be the chief occupation of His creation, it does not come naturally. It must be learned and practiced. Where better can this learning process begin than in the personal sanctuary of solitude?

The ideas shared in this book were tested not in the protected isolation of academia, but in the disorganized laboratory of real life. Most of the manuscript was written during a six-month period of "nomadic living" for our family. While we waited for a new house to be built, we moved five times, lived out of suitcases and boxes, and desperately missed the close proximity of friends, church, and school that we had previously enjoyed.

The fact that I was able to finish this book during such a difficult time attests to the beauty of the functioning body of Christ. First, there was the woman who graciously transcribed my husband's messages, which I tapped heavily as a source. Then there was the woman who chose not to teach a Bible study so that she could care for my children while I wrote. As I approached my final deadline, others prepared meals for us so that I wouldn't have to quit writing to cook. Still others offered constant support and encouragement through their notes and calls.

Then there were Mom and Dad. What would I have done without their help? They lovingly entertained Todd, my four-year-old son, for weeks at a time while I "ran away" to write. My mother-in-law, too, gave the kids the extra loving attention that only a grandma can give, which helped to make up for the limited attention they received from me.

Though I am a pastor's wife, I do not fit the stereotype that many associate with that role. I don't teach Sunday School or lead the choir. Nor do I serve on church committees or direct the Women's Ministry. I am not opposed to doing those things, but I am simply not gifted to do them. God has given me the ability and the desire to sit in the privacy of my at-home office and write. I thank Him for giving me that ability, and I thank the people of our church for giving me the freedom to use it.

This book is neither a textbook nor a doctrinal study. It is, rather, a record of my personal journey into the realm of worship. I offer it not as a means of flaunting my expertise, for I have none. I offer it more as a thank-you gift to God for giving me the matchless blessing of His presence and His love. If this material is helpful to others, it is because of the gracious work of the Holy Spirit, who alone has the power to bring truth to bear on our lives.

To my husband Bill

Without him, I could not have written this book. He calmed me down when I threatened to throw the manuscript in the fireplace. He constantly affirmed my abilities. And he gently reminded me to practice what I preach, to read what I was writing, and to *worship, worship, worship*!

For that, and for all else he has done for me, I thank him.

1
Attitudes of Worship

I could hardly wait for my weekly horseback ride. How I looked forward to that break from an otherwise routine schedule. The snow-dressed trees laden with shimmering icicles, the occasional deer that peaked timidly around the tree trunks, the sunshine that filtered through the branches, the exhilarating surge of speed and grace that glowed from the powerful horse—I could already see the beauty and feel the excitement that the morning ride would bring.

Only when I raised the window shade to let the morning ease its way in did I realize that the weather had not cooperated with my plans. Gentle raindrops steadily tapped the window, occasionally turning to tiny bits of hail. Too well I knew that the icy trails would be closed to an inexperienced rider like myself. The soupy grey sky mirrored my deflated mood.

The Inevitable Mundane

For me, much of life is filled with the mundane—cooking, cleaning, scrubbing, shopping, mending, doing laundry, etc. As a homemaker, wife, mother, and writer, I daily face those endless little tasks that simply *must* be done.

Of course, that is not *all* there is to my life. There are also the special people and places and times that are anything but mundane. There is the quiet joy of knowing that my words or my services have ministered to a friend. There is the pleasure of perseverance—the welcome knowledge that a job has been done well, a deadline has been met, and the "powers that be" are pleased. There are the longed-for moments when love is shared.

These are the moments of which our dreams and memories are made. But they are, nonetheless, just moments—moments defined and separated by the mundane.

It was to the mundane that my attention was drawn on that dreary, rainy day in February when my plans for fun were so abruptly changed. I decided to devote my unplanned free time to the healthy stack of crinkled shirts that had not yet made their way to the ironing board. With a children's tape playing in the background and a four-year-old driver playing traffic jam with 13 trucks beneath my feet, I began the unwelcome task.

But a strange thing happened that morning. As I ironed the shirts, one after another, an amazing transformation began to take place in my mind. Since my son refused to switch tapes, I became a captive audience to a choir of children's voices. I was not paying great attention to their words, but my attention, or lack of it, made little difference. The power of music had already begun its mysterious work. Soon I was silently mouthing the words, and before long I was singing right out loud. And just as those words had crept unexpectedly to my lips, so they began an unanticipated journey into my mind and soul.

"Jesus . . . beautiful Saviour. . . ." As I sang those words I was irresistibly drawn into their meaning, and gradually my outlook changed. The dreariness of the day didn't matter anymore, nor did the disappointment of broken plans or the "boringness" of mundane tasks. My hands still pushed the iron back and forth, carefully pressing neat creases into man-sized shirt-sleeves. But my mind had answered a loftier call, and in answering that call I stumbled upon a transcendent joy.

In that brief moment I became a worshiper, and in my worship I was changed. I felt as if I had come in direct contact with the eternal. *My* spirit had touched *The* Spirit. I was in the presence of the Almighty and there was no place else that I wanted to be.

The Missing Piece

Does that sound a bit extreme? A little too mystical for you?

A short time ago such words would have sounded very strange to me too. Though I grew up in a Christian home, I never learned anything about *true* worship. In retrospect, I realize that I assumed that because I was a Christian, I was automatically a worshiper. In a sense, of course, that is true, for in identifying myself as a Christian, I acknowledged my allegiance and submission to the true God. I failed, however, to move from that vague and passive acknowledgment of God into a more clearly defined attitude of worship. I didn't view worship as a meaningful activity in which I should consciously engage.

Throughout those years I was aware of a nagging anxiety and restlessness in my Christian life, but I was never able to determine the source of the problem. I was afraid that I was displeasing God, that I was concentrating on nonessentials, that I had somehow missed the *key* to Christian living. Only in the last two years have I learned that the key is worship.

Celebrate!

Unfortunately, the word *worship* brings to many people's minds nothing more than the elements of the liturgy to which they are accustomed. They may think of robed choirs, candles, and stained glass, or of the sacraments of communion and baptism, or even of the specific readings, hymns, and rituals that accompany worship in their particular churches. But while liturgies and rituals may symbolize and express the worship of our hearts, true worship is far more than these external elements.

Worship means "to attribute worth" to something or someone. For Christians, the object of our worship is God; so true Christian worship is an active response to God whereby we declare His worth. In worship, we consciously focus our attention on *who* God is and *what* He has done and promises to do in the future. Worship is not just a carefully designed ritual, nor is it simply a feeling or a mood or a passive acknowledgment of God's existence and authority. It is an active, directed, conscious, meaningful *celebration* of who God is.

"And though you have not seen Him, you love Him, and though you do not see Him now, but believe in Him, you *greatly rejoice with joy inexpressible and full of glory*" (1 Peter 1:8).*

That is true worship. Not a solemn duty, but a high privilege and a matchless delight. "Shout *joyfully* to the Lord. . . . Come before Him with *joyful* singing" (Ps. 100:1-2). These verses paint for us the picture of a joyous celebration—a celebration of our great and glorious God!

Reverence

It is, however, a celebration that is bathed in reverence. The psalmist says, "Worship the Lord with *reverence,* and rejoice with *trembling*" (Ps. 2:11). "At Thy holy temple I will *bow in reverence* for Thee" (5:7). Lest we conclude that such concern for reverence was limited to Old Testament times, the writer to the Hebrews says, "Therefore, since we receive a kingdom which cannot be shaken, let us show gratitude, by which we may offer to God an acceptable service with *reverence and awe*; for our God is a consuming fire" (Heb. 12:28-29).

Reverence, trembling, bow, awe—these are not words that we usually associate with a celebration. But when the object of our celebration is the God "greatly *feared* in the council of the holy ones, and *awesome* above all those who are around Him" (Ps. 89:7), our celebration must not be careless or lighthearted. Yes, we are called to celebrate. Yes, we are called to rejoice with "joy inexpressible." But we are to do so with reverence.

To illustrate reverence, let me relate an experience my husband had some years ago. During a 1968 summer vacation in Washington, D.C., Bill and a friend found themselves caught up in the social phenomenon called Resurrection City. Blacks and other oppressed minorities had descended upon Washington by the thousands. With tents, sleeping bags, and other necessary supplies, they camped across from the Washington Monument to protest the injustice of oppression.

---

*Hereafter, all italicized words in Scripture verses are used for author's emphasis.

Their objective was to raise the consciousness level of the American people to the plight of the poor. With this goal in mind, they sang, they held rallies, and they joined hands in symbolic gestures of support and unity. In spite of the seriousness of their goal, the warmth of their unity led to an almost festive atmosphere.

This peaceful display of camaraderie and unity was disturbed only on those isolated occasions when mounted policemen rode through Resurrection City. What a transformation took place then, as the pent-up hostilities brought about by years of oppression spewed forth in acts of bitterness and violence. Politicians too, who had to drive by the Washington Monument, proved to be easy targets for the hostilities of the assembled poor. Mud balls, eggs, tomatoes, bricks—all these became the ammunition of hatred.

Then, in the middle of this bedlam, word came that Bobby Kennedy had been assassinated. That news brought grief throughout the country, but in Resurrection City it brought an even graver grief. To the oppressed of Resurrection City, Bobby Kennedy had been a significant source of much needed hope. They had been clinging to the optimistic expectation that he would have the power and the desire to work against oppression. Now he was dead.

During the following two days an invisible cloud hung over Resurrection City, but the same basic pattern of life continued. There were the signs of comfortable unity, broken only by the occasional outbursts of directed animosity. Then late in the afternoon of the third day, a dramatic change took place. Suddenly there were no more frisbees, no more jokes, no more songs—and no more animosity. People quietly took their places on the sides of the street and waited. They talked in hushed tones and watched until they could see the headlights of the vehicles in the approaching motorcade. The body of Bobby Kennedy was being taken past the Washington Monument, through Resurrection City, and on to Arlington National Cemetery.

As the procession passed by, blacks stood next to whites, politicians stood next to the leaders of the protest movement, and policemen stood next to those who had hurled rocks at them the day before. There was no heavy-handed official commanding people to be quiet or stand still. Everyone understood that the moment demanded silence.

True reverence is that natural silence, that sense of awe, that healthy fear that for some inexplicable reason seems appropriate to the occasion. At funerals no one has to tell us the rules. There is something about the situation that demands that we take it very seriously. When we see a scene of breathtaking beauty—an ocean sunset or a snowcapped mountain—we don't try to capture it in words. We know that nothing we could say would adequately express the majesty of the sight, so we willingly appreciate it in reverential silence.

It is that way in worship. When we come before God, we come before a Being so mighty in power, in majesty, and in beauty that the only fitting attitude is one of sincere reverence. Without that attitude we can't be true worshipers.

"The Lord is in His holy temple," says the Prophet Habakkuk. "Let all the earth be silent before Him" (Hab. 2:20, NIV). *Be quiet!* he says. *Don't say a thing!* Don't rush into God's presence with a heart and mind spilling forth thoughtless words. Still your mind. Quiet your heart. Realize what it means to stand in the presence of the Holy God.

Submission

Our celebration of God begins with reverence—with silence, with awe, with a holy fear—but it doesn't end there. The natural outgrowth of sincere reverence is submission. When I quiet myself before God and concentrate on *who* He is and *what* He has done for me, I can in good conscience do nothing but submit to Him. If I have really caught a glimpse of His majesty, His power, His mercy, His loving-kindness, and all else that He is, I will be irresistibly drawn to commit myself to pleasing and obeying Him.

In Gethsemane, Jesus said, "Not My will, but Thine be done" (Luke 22:42). Like Him, we too must give voice to our willingness to cast off our own personal aspirations and selfish desires, and consciously submit ourselves to God's designs.

"Humble yourselves, therefore, under the mighty hand of God" (1 Peter 5:6). That is what we do in worship. First we stand silent before God in reverence. Then we bow down before Him in humble submission. We acknowledge and welcome His authority, and commit ourselves to faithful obedience. If we worship Him from any other position, we are offering Him nothing more than an empty ritual. We are offering Him the outer garment of worship, but not the heart—not the essence—of true worship.

Exaltation

With this foundation of reverence and submission firmly established, we can then move on to the next element of worship—exaltation. While reverence and submission are basically passive responses, exaltation is an active response whereby we audibly, or in our thoughts, "lift up" the Lord. *Exalt* means "to raise high; to elevate; to dignify; to magnify; to extol; to glorify; to lift up with joy and pride." When we exalt the Lord, we praise His dignity, His power, and His attributes. We thank Him for what He has done and express our joy at being His children.

"Oh give thanks to the Lord, call upon His name; make known His deeds among the peoples. Sing to Him, sing praises to Him; speak of all His wonders. Glory in His holy name; let the heart of those who seek the Lord be glad" (Ps. 105:1-3). These verses are rich with meaning for the worshiper. *Give thanks, make known His deeds, sing praises, speak of His name, be glad*—all of these are elements of exaltation and commands repeated throughout the Psalms.

The New Testament reiterates this theme. "Through Him then let us continually offer up a sacrifice of praise to God, that is, the fruit of lips that give thanks to His name" (Heb. 13:15). Don't just praise Him now and then on special occasions or in carefully created settings. Worship Him always, everywhere. Learn to live with a constant attitude of praise and thanksgiving.

A Personal Response

Not long ago I heard my four-year-old son say to his friend, "My mommy's nice, isn't she?" It was just one short sentence uttered in the peculiar dialect common only to four-year-olds, but what joy those words brought to me!

I will never tire of overhearing those spontaneous praises, nor of feeling little arms encircling my neck, accompanied by an unprovoked, "I love you, Mommy." Why? Because I *love* my children! In fact, I love them so much that what they think of me is just about the most important thing in the world. I receive a tremendous amount of pleasure from knowing that they love me and appreciate the things that I do for them. My deep love for them makes their responses very important.

Isn't it the same with God? Though I do not claim to completely understand why God desires our worship, I'm certain that part of His reason is the pure joy of hearing our heartfelt response to His unfathomable love. He has created and redeemed us. He has called us by name and loved us with an everlasting love. Shouldn't we expect Him to desire our loving response?

For 10 weeks last summer we rented a tiny knotty pine cottage in Michigan. Tucked away in the middle of a wooded lot that overlooked the sandy beaches of Lake Michigan, it was a perfect place to relax, play, read, write—and enjoy the beauty of the summer. During our first five weeks there, Bill was still living and working in Chicago. Though he was just three hours away by car, his schedule prohibited him from making the trip as often as he would have liked. Consequently, the kids and I saw him only two or three times during that period—on rushed one-day trips.

In between times, because I was enjoying a very relaxed schedule, I had plenty of time to think about Bill—to remember special things he had done for me and to appreciate his role in my life. Often my thoughts led to such feelings of love that I just had to call and tell him how I felt. Since our tiny cottage had no phone, I had to "buy some time" on a neighbor's phone. Though that arrangement was far from convenient, the calls were well worth the effort and the cost.

So it is with worship. As my telephone calls to Bill were prompted not by duty but by love, so our offerings of worship should be a means of expressing not just our resigned obedience, but our sincere love and admiration for our gracious Father.

In reverence, we acknowledge God's worth; in submission, we acknowledge His authority. In exaltation, we lift Him up with our expressions of adoration. That, in summary, is *true* worship. It is not a dutiful homage to a tyrant God, nor a means of gaining God's favor, but rather a natural response to the favor already graciously bestowed upon us by our great and glorious Lord.

2
Why Worship?

For years as I sat in doctors' waiting rooms or stood in grocery checkout lines, I studied the behavior of young mothers with a curious mixture of amusement and disbelief. The more I watched, the more confused I became.

I couldn't understand that dreamy, fixed gaze that a new mom focused on the tiny bundle cradled in her arms. Nor could I understand how she maintained a gracious spirit while she inched her way through a crowded store, her shoulders drooping under the awkward weight of an overflowing diaper bag.

Equally mysterious to me was the mom who joyfully welcomed a toddler onto her lap for a quick "cuddle," knowing that a mere 30 seconds of this shared affection would leave her new skirt hopelessly wrinkled, and her favorite earring lost forever in the vicious jungle of the shag carpet.

And why did young moms always have to talk about their children? Where did they get this irrepressible need to share so many "cute" stories and "adorable" photos that looked (to me anyway) just like the stories and photos every other mother shared?

Even harder for me to comprehend was how mothers could tolerate their children's constant interruptions, and how they could stand to arrange their daily schedules around naps and snacks and piano lessons and birthday parties. How could they maintain their joy when they were so often housebound by their kids' viruses and sprained ankles and runny noses? How did they hang on to their sanity?

Motherhood looked to me more like a drudgery than a delight, and mother love seemed more like a duty than a natural and spontaneous response.

During the past seven years, however, I have learned that my failure to understand "the joys of motherood" and "the depths of mother love" was based solely on my lack of personal experience. I was looking at it only from the outside. I failed to comprehend mother love because it had not yet touched my own heart and soul. I was a spectator rather than a participant.

The same, I have found, is true of worship. When I viewed worship from the outside, it didn't make sense to me. I couldn't see its value. I couldn't comprehend how otherwise practical people could justify the time and energy that worship demanded. With all the real, tangible needs in this world, how could they justify such a "nonproductive" activity as worship?

Maybe David had time to write psalms, and sing and dance in celebration of his God, but I certainly didn't. In my world there were kids starving and countries at war and men and women going to hell. In my church there were sick moms who needed meals, lonesome seniors who needed friends, and baby Christians who needed nurturing. In my home there were clothes to be washed, floors to be swept, and, of course, relationships to be preserved. It took time and energy to meet all these needs and fill all these roles. How could God add one more demand to the list—and such a nebulous, intangible one at that?

Besides, I thought, *what kind of God would seek—even demand—our worship?* An egotist? An insecure tyrant? I know those words sound blasphemous, but for me, the misunderstanding was real. I could not comprehend such a God.

Getting on the Inside
How have I come to understand this mystery called worship? Simply by getting on the *inside.* By becoming a worshiper. I only

came to understand mothering by becoming a mother. Likewise, I have only come to understand worship by worshiping.

When I saw my daughter at the instant of her birth, I no longer had to wonder about mother love. There before me was bone of my bone, flesh of my flesh—living, breathing, beautiful, and perfect. I didn't have to wonder if I should love her, or try to psyche myself up to love her. Love was my natural, spontaneous response.

When, in an attitude of true worship, I first caught a glimpse of the real God—the holy, majestic, loving, and glorious God of Scripture—I no longer had to wonder about worship. I no longer questioned its meaning or value. Nor did I question the character of a God who would desire my worship. In my glimpse of the true God, I knew immediately that there simply was no other appropriate response. Why He *wants* my worship I don't fully understand. But that He *deserves* it is beyond my doubts. He is absolutely and undeniably worthy. And that is what matters.

My first real "tug" in the direction of worship came at a retreat where my husband traced the subject of worship through Scripture. How I had read the Bible for 20 years without realizing the continual theme of worship, I don't know—but somehow I managed to do it. As I listened to my husband speak, my eyes were opened to something so obvious, and yet so fresh and new, that I couldn't help but respond with enthusiasm.

Worship is a constant theme in Scripture. Woven throughout the course of recorded history are God's commands to worship, His affirmation of true worship, and His chastisement of nonworshipers.

From the Beginning

At Creation, the heavenly beings were involved in worship. "Where were you when I laid the earth's foundation . . . while the morning stars sang together and all the angels shouted for joy?" (Job 38:4, 7, NIV)

Somewhat later, when God gave Moses the Ten Commandments, what commandment topped the list? "You shall have no other gods before Me" (Ex. 20:3). In effect, God was saying,

"Don't worship or honor anyone else. *I* am the One. *I* am the Lord. Worship *Me!*"

The second commandment continues the thought. "You shall not make for yourself an idol, or any likeness of what is in heaven above or on the earth beneath or in the water under the earth. You shall not worship them or serve them; for I, the Lord your God am a jealous God" (vv. 4-5). In this passage God warns us against trying to reduce the totality of who He is to a piece of stone or wood. It is a sacrilege to try to capsulize His essence, or to produce with our hands a facsimile of who He is.

The third commandment takes this concept one step further. "You shall not take the name of the Lord your God in vain, for the Lord will not leave him unpunished who takes His name in vain" (v. 7). Just as we should not try to reduce His essence by representing Him with a graven image, so we should not reduce His holiness and majesty by taking His name lightly. We must be careful how we talk about God and how we use His name.

Another scriptural theme related to worship is the Old Testament sacrificial system. As the altars were built, the animals slain, and the fires lit, the hearts of the people bowed in humility. And as the smoke rose upward and drifted beyond the range of human sight, it presented a vivid image of sincere worship flowing from human hearts to the very heart of God.

Like the sacrificial system, the tabernacle was also a significant element in Old Testament worship. In chapter after chapter, Scripture gives detailed instructions regarding the construction and layout of the tabernacle. Everything in it was designed to emphasize the importance of worship. Located in the center of the camp, it was used not as a gathering place or a meeting place, but strictly for worship. Everything about it attested to the priority of worship in the Israelites' lives.

Worship Defiled

The Bible speaks not only of the priority of worship, but also of God's judgment against those who defile worship. As early as the Book of Genesis we see the awful distortion of God's perfect plan for His creation.

In perfect fellowship with God, Adam and Eve enjoyed communion with their Father and in submission obeyed His every command—until they fell prey to Satan's clever scheme. "Eat of the tree," said the serpent, "and you will be like God. You won't have to bow down to Him. You won't have to worship Him as Creator and Lord. Go ahead. Eat!" When Adam and Eve bought Satan's lie and sought to be like God, they ceased to worship Him. And when they ceased to worship, they yielded to sin and were forced to leave the Garden (Gen. 3:1-24).

Their offspring too knew the importance of worship, but like their parents they perverted it. When Cain produced an unacceptable sacrifice and Abel an acceptable one, Cain, in a jealous rage, killed his brother. Distinguishing himself as the world's first murderer, Cain was cursed by God and driven from his home and family (4:1-12).

Sometime later the Israelites, yielding to the heathen practice of idol worship, created a golden calf to represent their God. God's wrath was so kindled against them that He contemplated the total destruction of the nation. Mercifully He minimized the outpouring of His righteous anger and spared the vast majority of offenders (Ex. 32:1-29), but still His point was clear.

The young priests Nadab and Abihu, sons of Aaron, were judged and killed because they failed to follow exactly God's prescribed plan for worship (Lev. 10:1-2). Likewise, Uzzah died because he ignored God's specific guidelines for transporting the Ark of the Covenant (2 Sam. 6:1-7).

The Old Testament traces the rise and fall of the kings of Israel. Those kings who rebuilt the altars, removed the idols from the temple, and established disciplined worship of the true God, prospered. The hand of God was upon them and His blessing was evident throughout the entire nation. But those kings who refused to worship the true God were doomed to failure. Disaster followed on the heels of disaster, not only for the evil kings, but for the entire nation.

The Book of Malachi is a thorough indictment of the nonworshiping Israelites. " 'A son honors his father, and a servant his master. Then if I am a Father, where is My honor? And if I am

a Master, where is My respect?' says the Lord of hosts to you,
O priests who despise My name" (Mal. 1:6). Here God accuses
the priests—the very people chosen to lead the nation in worship—of disrespect toward Himself.

Later God accused them of defiling the altar. When they asked
how they had defiled it, He replied, "But when you present the
blind for sacrifice, is it not evil? And when you present the lame
and sick, is it not evil? Why not offer it to your governor? Would
he be pleased with you? Or would he receive you kindly?" (v. 8)
While the levitical law made it clear that only unblemished animals could be offered for sacrifice, the Israelites decided to revise
that law. Keeping the best animals for themselves, they offered
to God their sick and injured ones. Some even offered animals
that had been stolen (v. 13).

How despicable this was to God; He hated their shoddy sacrifices.
" 'Oh that there were one among you who would shut the gates,
that you might not uselessly kindle fire on My altar! *I am not
pleased with you,*' says the Lord of hosts, '*nor will I accept an
offering from you*' " (v. 10).

New Testament Theme

The New Testament continues the theme of worship. Seeking the
Baby Jesus, the magi asked, "Where is He who has been born
King of the Jews? For we saw His star in the east, and have come
to *worship* Him" (Matt. 2:2). Later, "they came into the house
and saw the Child with Mary His mother; and they fell down and
worshiped Him; and opening their treasures they presented to
Him gifts of gold and frankincense and myrrh" (v. 11).

Likewise, when the shepherds saw Jesus, they responded with
worship. "And the shepherds went back, glorifying and praising
God for all that they had heard and seen, just as had been told
them" (Luke 2:20).

In the record of Jesus' wilderness temptation, we read that
Satan said to Jesus, "I will give You all this domain and its glory;
for it has been handed over to me, and I give it to whomever I
wish. Therefore if You worship before me, it shall all be Yours"
(Luke 4:6-7). Jesus answered simply, "It is written, 'You shall

worship the Lord your God and serve Him only' " (v. 8). Imagine the irony of this situation. The only One truly worthy of worship was asked to worship the enemy!

Later on in the Gospel of Luke, we read the colorful account of Jesus' Triumphal Entry into Jerusalem just before His trial and arrest. "And as He was now approaching, near the descent of the Mount of Olives, the whole multitude of the disciples began to praise God joyfully with a loud voice for all the miracles which they had seen, saying, 'Blessed is the king who comes in the name of the Lord; peace in heaven and glory in the highest!' And some of the Pharisees in the multitude said to Him, 'Teacher, rebuke Your disciples.' And He answered and said, 'I tell you, if these become silent, the stones will cry out!' " (19:37-40) Jesus *deserved* to be worshiped. If the people refused to do it, the stones would take up the cry!

Continuing through the New Testament, we find the early church gathering together regularly to "praise God" (Acts 2:47). We read the apostle's exhortation to the Roman Christians to offer their lives as a "living and holy sacrifice, acceptable to God, which is your spiritual service of *worship*" (Rom. 12:1). In Hebrews we are told to "continually offer up a sacrifice of *praise* to God" (Heb. 13:15). And Peter reminds us to "*proclaim the excellencies* of Him who has called you out of darkness into His marvelous light" (1 Peter 2:9). All of these statements are clear commands to worship.

Our Eternal Occupation

Our *ultimate* priority—worship—is also an *unending* priority. While our daily tasks and responsibilities are temporal, our call to worship is eternal.

In the Book of Revelation, we read of the heavenly creatures surrounding the throne of God. "And day and night they do not cease to say, 'Holy, Holy, Holy, is the Lord God, the Almighty, who was and who is and who is to come.' And when the living creatures give glory and honor and thanks to Him who sits on the throne, to Him who lives forever and ever, the twenty-four elders will fall down before Him who sits on the throne, and will worship

Him who lives forever and ever, and will cast their crowns before the throne, saying, 'Worthy art Thou, our Lord and our God, to receive glory and honor and power; for Thou didst create all things, and because of Thy will they existed, and were created' " (Rev. 4:8-11).

From the foundation of the world, the heavenly beings have been engaged in worship, and throughout eternity, we too will join in their lofty call. We will see the Lord as He is, and our only response will be adoration and awe.

The Cart before the Horse

The Westminster Catechism says, "The chief end of man is to glorify God and enjoy Him forever." The writers of this catechism thoroughly studied the Bible and organized the basic scriptural themes into a respected presentation of systematic theology. Their answer to the age-old question of man's purpose was stated in unequivocal terms. Man was created to worship—to celebrate God.

With this truth in mind, can we doubt the importance of worship to God? Can we possibly justify nonworship?

Over the past several decades the church has managed to do just that. It has justified nonworship. How? By voicing the same objection that was raised in the beginning of this chapter. "How can we take time out to worship when there is so much service to be done?" Our church leaders may not put it in those exact words. But their silence on the subject of worship, combined with their repeated challenges to greater service, lead us to believe that our first and primary spiritual priority is to become busy for God.

So that's what we do. We become *doers* of the Word. We become committed. Dedicated. *Driven.*

And in the process we put the proverbial cart before the horse. We run helter skelter through a maze of "good" activities, never taking time to center in on the "best." We expend all our energies on the occupations of our hands, and forget to nourish the occupations of our hearts and minds. We rush around in God's presence and parade before Him our many accomplishments, never stopping long enough to be silent before Him in reverential awe. We become servants who don't know how to worship.

In his brilliant book on worship, A.W. Tozer writes, "We're here to be worshipers first and workers only second. We take a convert and immediately make a worker out of him. God never meant it to be so. God meant that a convert should learn to be a worshiper, and after that he can learn to be a worker" (*Worship: The Missing Jewel of the Evangelical Church,* Christian Publications, Inc., p. 14).

Richard Foster says, "If the Lord is to be Lord, worship must have priority in our lives. The first commandment of Jesus is 'Love the Lord your God with all your heart, and with all your soul, and with all your mind, and with all your strength' (Mark 12:30). The divine priority is worship first, service second. Our lives are to be punctuated with praise, thanksgiving, and adoration. Service flows out of worship. Service as a substitute for worship is idolatry. Activity may become the enemy of adoration" (*Celebration of Discipline,* Harper and Row, p. 140).

As a pastor's wife, I am in a good position to see the needs of the church body, and my natural tendency is to respond to as many needs as I can. *Perhaps I can rearrange my schedule so I can baby-sit for that woman tomorrow. Maybe if I hurry I can prepare a meal for that family whose mother is ill. If I can find someone to baby-sit my children, maybe I can go to that special meeting.*

On and on it goes. And as my schedule gets busier and busier, my priorities move farther and farther away from God's ordained pattern of worship first, service second. My private times of prayer and Bible study become more infrequent, and my mind becomes less and less devoted, less and less capable of thoughtful meditation on the majesty of my God. I become a servant who does not worship.

It's tempting to flaunt our busy schedules—until we realize that there is nothing noble about frenzied activity. Will God be pleased when we stand before Him someday and say, "I know I never learned to be a worshiper, but look how much I did for You"? Will He be pleased? Scripture shouts an emphatic No!

Those of us who sincerely want to please the living God and who desire to find that ultimate purpose for which we were created, have no choice. We *must* become worshipers.

3
Our "Aweful" God

Imagine the Apostle Paul as he walked through the city of Athens. Up and down the dusty streets he traveled, overhearing the animated conversations of the self-proclaimed philosophers and gazing sadly at the vast array of man-made idols. Athens was the home of the famed Areopagus, where the latest in sophisticated ideas were paraded in much the same way that Paris parades her new spring fashions. There Paul saw the well-known altar which bore these words of acknowledged ignorance: "To an Unknown God" (Acts 17:16-23).

It was in Athens that Paul delivered his famous "Sermon on Mars Hill" (vv. 22-31). Invited to the Areopagus by a group of philosophers intrigued by his proclamation of "strange deities" (v. 18), Paul shared with them the identity of the unknown God whom they worshiped in ignorance. He told them about the God of Scripture, the "God who made the world and all things in it" (v. 24), the God in whom "we live and move and exist" (v. 28), the God who "is now declaring to men that all everywhere should repent" (v. 30). He taught them also of Jesus, whom God had raised from the dead, and at that "some began to sneer, but others said, 'We shall hear you again concerning this' " (v. 32). Still others joined Paul and believed.

Paul was provoked as he walked through the streets of Athens by the depth of ignorance that existed even in the midst of such extensive knowledge. But, I wonder, would Paul be any less provoked if he could walk unnoticed up and down the aisles of our churches, or if he could miraculously peer inside our minds and glimpse the god that we worship? Would he once again despair at the poverty of our knowledge of God? I'm afraid that Paul would probably preach again the "Sermon on Mars Hill" for the benefit of the multitude of religious people who still worship the "unknown god."

"God is spirit, and those who worship Him must worship in spirit and truth" (John 4:24). To worship God in *spirit,* our worship must originate from within. It is not merely a matter of externals—of being in the right place, saying the right words, going through the right ritual. Rather, it is a matter of heart—of sincerity, love, and personal devotion. To worship God in *truth,* our worship must be based on an accurate knowledge of who God is.

The Athenians focused on ideas, but not on truth. They sought meaning in the interchange of *human* thought, while they ignored the truth revealed in *divine* thought. Many Christians today are doing the same thing. They worship, but they worship without the knowledge of objective truth. They don't really know the facts about God.

The ancient Athenians acknowledged their ignorance. In order to protect themselves from possibly offending an unknown god by failing to worship him, they erected their famed altar in his honor. Most 20th century Christians are, in contrast to the Athenians, unaware of their ignorance. They know there is but one God, and that He alone is worthy to be worshiped, so they acknowledge His existence and go through the motions of worship, sincerely believing that the god they worship is the God revealed in Scripture.

But is He? Do we really know the truth about God? Or have we concocted our own gods, based on snatches of biased information, personal experience, tradition, and isolated Scripture lifted out of context? Is the God we worship the holy and majestic God of Scripture, or is He a puny figment of our imaginations?

My Unworthy God

Growing up in a stable, evangelical church, I assumed that I had a healthy image of God. I knew Him as Creator and Sustainer of the universe and as the Lord of my life. I accepted His existence and His authority as indisputable. I considered service on behalf of His kingdom the loftiest of goals, and I took seriously my commitment to obey Him as best I could. Consequently, when I learned about the importance of disciplined and heartfelt worship, I decided immediately that I had to become a more devoted worshiper. If worship was God's grandest plan for His creation, then I wanted to worship!

Timidly, cautiously, I began to write prayers and personal psalms of worship in my journal. In reverential silence I turned my thoughts consciously toward God, and with my written words I offered my confession, my submission, and my inexperienced attempts at exaltation. I was a novice, but at least I was heading in the right direction. I was learning to worship. And I was conscientiously committed to my new discipline.

My commitment, however, began to waver. I really *wanted* to be a worshiper, but so many questions crowded into my mind. Who was this God I was worshiping? Why did He want my worship? Did He really deserve it? I knew I should be able to shout an unequivocal Yes! to the last question, but in all honesty I couldn't.

God, as I perceived Him, did not call forth my worship. I *wanted* Him to. I *wanted* the majesty of His being to drive me to enthusiastic, heartfelt worship. But it didn't. I remained unmoved. Worship became a chore, an "ought." It was something I had to do simply because it was *expected*.

Fortunately, I had learned enough about true worship to know that my heartless, empty words were not acceptable. I couldn't continue in the same pattern and hope to please the Lord. I had to find out what was wrong. Why was I having so much trouble becoming a worshiper?

J. B. Phillips says, "Many men and women today are living, often with inner dissatisfaction, without any faith in God at all. This is not because they are particularly wicked or selfish or, as the old-fashioned would say, 'godless,' but because they have not found with their adult minds a God big enough to 'account for' life, big enough to 'fit in with' the new scientific age, big enough to command their highest admiration and respect, and consequently their willing cooperation" (*Your God Is Too Small*, Mac-Millan Publishing Co., p. 8).

Was this my problem? Had I failed to find a God big enough to command my highest admiration and respect? Big enough to be worthy of my worship?

Knowing that the Psalms provide the clearest examples of true biblical worship, I began to read them consistently every day. Over and over again I was impressed by the psalmists' commitment to worship. They bowed down in worship. They lifted their hands in worship. They danced and sang in worship. They even shouted in worship. Obviously, *they* had no lack of enthusiasm. They worshiped in the midst of joy and in sorrow, in the face of gain and of loss. They worshiped both when they were filled with confidence, and when they were afraid. They worshiped continually, it seemed, and in every kind of situation.

Unlike the God described by Phillips, the God of the psalmists was unquestionably "big enough to command their highest admiration and respect." He was lofty and majestic and worthy of their complete and unashamed devotion. Repeatedly their words expressed heartfelt praise and adoration. God was worthy and they wanted the world to know it!

What did David and the other psalmists know about God that I didn't know? I wondered. *What compelled them to be such worshipers?*

As I continued my daily reading, I searched for answers. The more I read, the more clearly I saw that David's God is truly a God beautiful in His majesty and awesome in His power. "The Lord reigns, let the peoples tremble," wrote David (Ps. 99:1). With those words he revealed his own attitude of absolute respect toward God. Time after time he acknowledged the vast disparity between God's perfection and man's sin, between God's strength and man's weakness. In humility, David openly confessed his own sins and begged for God's forgiveness.

On the other hand, David possessed a remarkable confidence in his standing before this awesome, holy God. He came boldly into God's presence, as if he knew beyond question that God would accept and love and bless him. God was David's friend, his strength, his protector, his joy, his shelter, and his refuge.

David bowed before God in holy fear and trembling, and at the same time boldly entered His presence with unabashed confidence. *What a mystery,* I thought. *How could such opposing responses as fear and confidence be so inextricably bound together in one man's experience with God?*

The answer is simply that David knew the *true* God. He had a clear and balanced portrait of the God revealed in Scripture. The God revealed in the real-life drama of history. The God who spoke and acted and manifested His power and glory in visible, tangible ways.

The Incomprehensible God Revealed

God is, by His nature, beyond the scope of human understanding and knowledge. He transcends our sphere of existence. His infinite character refuses to be contained by our finite understanding.

Our human tendency is to reduce and simplify that which is beyond us so that we can understand and explain it. We *must,* however, resist doing that to God. If we reduce Him to the level of our understanding, if we simplify Him so that our finite minds can contain Him, we have created a false god—a god no less empty than the idols carved by Athenian hands. To our finite minds, God is and ever shall be incomprehensible.

God's incomprehensibility does not, however, mean that He is utterly unknowable. While there will always remain a secret, mysterious dimension to God that we do not know, there *is much that we can know.* God has revealed Himself clearly, if not fully, through general revelation (evidence from nature) and verbal revelation (evidence from the Bible). If we are willing to steep our minds in this revealed truth, we can know the real God, and in that conscious knowing, we can worship Him in spirit and in truth.

Nothing will affect the whole of our lives, both in this world and in the world to come, as much as our concept of God. Our attitudes toward ourselves, toward others, toward creation, toward history, toward the future, toward our goals, our careers, and our relationships will be influenced by how we view God. Is He a benevolent old grandfather, just waiting to heap blessings upon us? Is He the ultimate cosmic ogre, ruling with an iron thumb? Is He alive, but distant? Is He predictable or unpredictable? Personal or impersonal? Should we fear Him? Should we love Him? How does He behave? How can we describe Him?

In Scripture we can find answers to all these questions.

The First Cause

We learn first that God is *self-existent*. To the ancient philosopher, but also to any thinking man or woman of the 20th century, this must be the starting place. If this were all that we knew of our God, it would indeed set Him apart from all else. It is the most fundamental difference between God and all other creatures. He alone is *un*created. All else that exists or has ever existed is created. It received its being, its life, from something other than itself. Only our God has an existence dependent upon nothing else. He alone has within Himself the power of being.

For centuries, scholars have discussed the source of life, of energy, of motion. All around us we see evidence of a dynamic, changing, moving world. We see it in the breath of life that fills the lungs of a newborn child. We see it in the constant orbit of the planets, and in the wild gyrations of sub-atomic particles. We see it in the rise and fall of waves upon the ocean, in the random movement of leaves caught in the wind. We see it in the changing of the seasons and in the aging of a man. In all spheres of nature we see motion, energy, and life.

And where did it come from? From the living God, the God who always was and who forever will be. The God who is *eternal*. "Before the mountains were born, or Thou didst give birth to the earth and the world, even from everlasting to everlasting, Thou art God" (Ps. 90:2).

As His being knows no bounds of time, so His perfect character knows no bounds of limited degree. All that God is, He is to the fullest. "Can you discover the depths of God? Can you discover the limits of the Almighty? It is high as the heavens, what can you do? Deeper than Sheol, what can you know? Its measure is longer than the earth, and broader than the sea" (Job 11:7-9). God is *infinite,* without limit. Therefore, all that flows from Him is likewise without limit. When we speak of human love, we speak of a love that knows limits, a love that can be stretched to the point of destruction. But God's love knows no such weakness; His love has no breaking point. Like all His attributes, it enjoys the limitless freedom of His divine infinitude.

The Great "Omni"

Not only is our God self-existent, eternal, and infinite, but He is also *omniscient.* He has perfect knowledge. There is nothing that can be hidden from Him. Nothing surprises Him, nothing escapes His notice, nothing is beyond His grasp. Not a thought or motive of the human heart can be protected from His knowledge. "Thou hast placed our iniquities before Thee, our secret sins in the light of Thy presence," said Moses (Ps. 90:8). David said, "Even before there is a word on my tongue, behold, O Lord, thou dost know it all" (Ps. 139:4). For the Christian, this means that not one soiled particle of our inner lives can be hidden from the penetrating gaze of the Father. But even though He knows us through and through, He still loves us!

Living in a world rich with knowledge, we know that the accumulation of knowledge has no value for godliness in and of itself. But where knowledge is mixed with wisdom, there we find an individual whose value is beyond compare.

So it is with our God. His infinite storehouse of knowledge is bathed in the light of infinite wisdom. Such wisdom is not mere cunning and shrewdness, like that which can be attributed even to evil men; rather it is wisdom which is always opposed to the ways of Satan and fallen men.

All of God's acts are done in perfect wisdom, in a manner not to be improved upon by finite creatures. A.W. Tozer says, "Wisdom, among other things, is the ability to devise perfect ends and to achieve those ends by the most perfect means. It sees the end from the beginning, so there can be no need to guess or conjecture. Wisdom sees everything in focus, each in proper relation to all, and is thus able to work toward predestined goals with flawless precision" (*The Knowledge of the Holy,* Harper and Row, p. 66). What a comfort this is to the Christian. We can yield willingly to God's will, knowing that God sees "the whole picture" and can be trusted to guide our lives in a way that will uphold both His glory and our ultimate good.

"Ah Lord God! Behold, Thou hast made the heavens and the earth by Thy great power and by Thine outstretched arm! Nothing is too difficult for Thee" (Jer. 32:17). Here we see a further element of God's perfect character. His all-knowing wisdom is joined by His infinite power; our God is *omnipotent.* As with His knowledge, His power has no limits. Undoubtedly, we see now a limited display of God's power, only to the degree that our finite minds and bodies can grasp. But someday we shall see the full outpouring of His power.

It is because of this ultimate power that David wrote, "The Lord has established His throne in the heavens; and His sovereignty rules over all" (Ps. 103:19). God is not only omniscient and omnipotent. He is also *sovereign.* No one can hinder Him, compel Him, or stop Him. He is in total control. Though He has given man freedom within bounds, *His* freedom is boundless. He reigns supreme in the total course of human events.

Throughout Scripture we read of God's sovereignty, and though many people ignore it, one day it will be undeniable. At that time, in accordance with His wisdom and by His infinite power, God will bring about the ultimate overthrow of evil. Everyone will know that He is the absolute Sovereign. On that day, "every knee [shall] bow . . . and every tongue [shall] confess that Jesus Christ is Lord, to the glory of God the Father" (Phil. 2:10-11).

The all-knowing, all-powerful Ruler of the universe has yet another divine attribute—He is *omnipresent.* Not limited by space nor contained by boundaries, He is everywhere, all the time. "Do I not fill the heavens and the earth?" declares the Lord through the Prophet Jeremiah (Jer. 23:24). That seems simple enough, but this simple truth provides tremendous insight into God's involvement in the ongoing life of His creation.

The fact that God is omnipresent assures us that though He is the *ultimate* Sovereign, He is not a *distant* Sovereign. He does not sit on His throne and rule from afar, casually disinterested and hopelessly uninformed. On the contrary, everything that happens—every good deed done and every sin committed—occurs, as it were, right in front of the very throne of God.

Yes, our God is awesome in His infinite, eternal knowledge and power, but He is also *intimate*. He is separate from His creation, yet miraculously and undeniably intermingled with it. Herein lies the mystery and majesty of the Great Omni—our living God. He fills the farthest reaches of the universe with His unending presence while remaining close by the side of those who seek Him. He rules the remotest stars of heaven while searching out the deepest motives of the human soul.

The Sinless One

This ultimate Sovereign is also the epitome of moral excellence and purity. He is *holy*. He has *no* sin, *no* imperfection, *no* stain, *no* blemish, and *no* shadow. "Thine eyes are too pure to approve evil," says the Prophet Habakkuk, "and Thou canst not look on wickedness with favor" (Hab. 1:13). God does not conform to a standard of holiness. He *is* the standard. And by His standard shall all else be judged.

In His holiness God stands apart from man. He is terrifying to us, because we cannot imagine pure holiness. The blazing light of His holiness sears us. It binds us. It makes us want to cover up our nakedness, as Adam did in the garden (Gen. 3:10). We don't want to stand in the face of moral perfection, for there our sin is too vivid.

When Isaiah had his life-changing view of God's holiness, he cried, "Woe is me, for I am ruined! Because I am a man of unclean lips, and I live among a people of unclean lips, for my eyes have seen the King, the Lord of hosts" (Isa. 6:5). In that brief glimpse of God's holiness, Isaiah saw the reflected horror of his own sin—and he was shamed to the point of despair.

In all of God's attributes, but never less than in His holiness, we see the transcendence of God's nature. He is above us and apart from us. He is unique, unapproachable, and mysterious. In essence and in quality of being, He is so far beyond the created order that human thought cannot even imagine Him. And in that sense He is unknowable. Awesome. Incomprehensible. The Most High.

A Personal Visit

In Exodus 19 we are given a verbal picture of this awesome, incomprehensible, Most High God. The people of Israel are camped at the foot of Mount Sinai. God is preparing to reveal to Moses the Ten Commandments. Throughout the trip from Egypt to Sinai, Moses has been the liaison between God and the Children of Israel. When God wanted to communicate to His people, He met with Moses at the tent of meeting, gave him the message, then sent Moses out to communicate it. Likewise, when the people wanted to respond to God, they sent their messages to Him through Moses.

At this point, however, God is aware that some of the people doubt Moses' authenticity as a liaison. They wonder, *Is Moses really meeting with God? Has he really been chosen by God? Perhaps he is deceiving us. Perhaps he's making up these messages. Maybe we don't really have to listen to him.*

Before God gives the all-important commandments, He wants to make sure that His people have no doubts about Moses. He wants to make sure that they accept the commandments as the commandments of God. So He designs a plan to authenticate Moses' leadership.

"And the Lord said to Moses, 'Behold, I shall come to you in a thick cloud, in order that the people may hear when I speak with you, and may also believe in you forever' " (Ex. 19:9). The holy and awesome God of the universe is going to reveal Himself personally to the entire nation of Israel. Imagine the excitement and the anticipation—and the fear. Never in their lives have the people dreamed of such a dramatic revelation. They have been taught that they could not look on the glory of God and live. Yet God has now chosen to reveal His glory in a way that they can endure. He will veil His glory in a cloud. He will allow them to catch a glimpse of His glory, yet protect them from the overwhelming power of His presence.

When I was a little girl, I spent hours in the garage watching my father restore the bodies of old cars. It was his favorite hobby, but he always enjoyed a little company while he worked and I was a willing companion. I loved to watch him skillfully shape a piece of flat sheet metal into a graceful curve or a sharp angle. But I always knew that when he put on his safety glasses and picked up his welder's torch, it was time to turn my back and fix my gaze on something "safe." I couldn't look at the flame from the torch without burning my eyes.

That's the way it was for the people at Sinai. They couldn't look at the glory of God with the naked eye, so God veiled His glory. He used the cover of the clouds as a protective lens to shield their eyes. But even with such protection, there were conditions.

"Go to the people and consecrate them today and tomorrow, and let them wash their garments; and let them be ready for the third day, for on the third day the Lord will come down on Mount Sinai in the sight of all the people" (vv. 10-11). God's visit was not to be taken lightly. All the ceremonial cleansing of the levitical law had to be carried out.

Then necessary boundaries had to be established. "And you shall set bounds for the people all around, saying, 'Beware that you do not go up on the mountain or touch the border of it; whoever touches the mountain shall surely be put to death. No hand shall touch him, but he shall surely be stoned or shot through; whether beast or man, he shall not live.' When the ram's horn sounds a long blast, they shall come up to the mountain" (vv. 12-13). God in His holiness was about to descend upon that mountain; it could not be profaned by the careless, over-eager approach of sinful man.

As I read this passage, I can't help but remember my first viewing of "The Wizard of Oz." I can almost see Dorothy, the lion, the tin man, and the scarecrow as they tiptoe into the throne room of the great Oz. They don't know what to expect. They don't know who he is or what he's like. But they know that they're going to find out soon. Finally, they see the throne, and as they approach it, their hearts are thumping with fear, dread, anticipation, and excitement.

Surely that must have been how it was among the Israelites as they awaited the visitation of the veiled presence of God. They must have wondered, *What will He be like? What will He do?*

Finally, the day arrived. "So it came about on the third day, when it was morning, that there were thunder and lightning flashes and a thick cloud upon the mountain and a very loud trumpet sound, so that all the people who were in camp trembled. And Moses brought the people out of the camp to meet God, and they stood at the foot of the mountains" (vv. 16-17). As I write these words, my emotions churn as I experience vicariously the Israelites' mounting fear. Surely they knew it was no ordinary rain cloud that settled upon the mountain that morning, and the trumpet sound was no earthly sound. They trembled, for something extraordinary and awesome was happening.

I can envision the people slowly making their way to the mountain. Their fear holds them back, but God's command pushes them forward. "Come to the mountain," He said, and so they come. But no one is so bold as to push beyond the established boundary. There is no arrogance or irreverence in the camp that day.

"Now Mount Sinai was all in smoke because the Lord descended upon it in fire; and its smoke ascended like the smoke of a furnace, and the whole mountain quaked violently. When the sound of the trumpet grew louder and louder, Moses spoke and God answered him with thunder" (vv. 18-19).

Can you imagine this scene? The mountain is smothered in smoke, not just gentle puffs of smoke, but smoke as in a furnace—billowing, choking, giant clouds of smoke. By this time, the sound of the trumpet must be deafening, and the thunder is booming with the voice of God. The people tremble and the mountain quakes. This is a full-scale cosmic upheaval, and they are caught in the midst of it!

Then, right in the middle of this divine sound and light show, God calls Moses up to the mountain, instructs him to remind the people again not to "break through to the Lord to gaze," and then tells him to bring Aaron up with him. Moses does as God commands (vv. 20-25). He warns the people, brings Aaron up to the mountain, and then receives the commandments which he and Aaron later pass on to the people.

As we read this account, it's important to keep in mind that God was not staging an intentional or exhaustive power display. He wasn't pulling out the stops so the people could see the full extent of His might. Had He done so, He would have annihilated them on the spot. Instead, He was simply giving them a tiny glimpse of His being so that they would know that the true God was communing with Moses.

I have read this passage over and over, trying to grasp the full picture. I want to see in my mind's eye the smoke that billowed around the mountain. I want to hear the thunder and the sound of the trumpet. I want to feel the shiver of the mountain. I want to know why the people trembled in the veiled presence of God.

So often I have barged carelessly into God's presence without the holy fear and reverence that is due Him. So often I have esteemed Him lightly, forgetting that He is the God of holiness and splendor.

If I had to designate one chapter in this book as being the most important, it would undoubtedly be this one, for it is here, in our focus on the attributes of God, that true worship must begin. We will never be motivated to worship a "small god," but if we can catch even a glimpse of the great, almighty God of David we will find no other appropriate response. We will gladly join the throng of saints before us who have cried, "Great is the Lord, and greatly to be praised" (Ps. 96:4).

4
Our "Refuge" God

"Twins," the doctor said. "What a surprise!"

A surprise, yes, but not a very pleasant one. On another day, it would have been wonderful—a cause for celebration. But not on that day, for I already knew what the doctor was reluctant to say. Within the next few hours, these two tiny creatures would be born with no hope of living. They were big enough to be a picture of life, but not big enough to handle the realities of life.

Ah well, I had been through this before. At least I knew what to expect.

Several years earlier, I had been less prepared. When the doctor informed me that a miscarriage was inevitable, I comforted myself with the thought that this "thing" to be lost was not yet a form that had taken on the endearing characteristics of an irresistible newborn. It was just a mass of unhealthy tissue, a product of faulty conception, a mistake.

Yes, I had consciously prepared myself to see the "unshaped mass of tissue" that is the product of most miscarriages. But what I saw instead was the miniature, yet detailed form of a baby. Tiny arms and legs. Tiny fingers and toes. Tiny head bowed in the usual fetal position.

All the cool, analytical defenses with which I had been protecting myself crumbled immediately in a flood of tears. Not once

43

during the hours of fever and labor had I allowed myself to think of this experience as "losing a baby." Yet there he was—my tiny little boy who for some unknown reason was taken from this world before he had even tasted of life.

I remembered the joy that had accompanied my daughter's birth. She, who had but moments before been a part of my own body, had suddenly become fully alive on her own. How miraculous!

But how different it was with this little boy. There was no joy. There was only the piercing awareness that in my brief viewing of his lifeless body, I had somehow come to know him, and in that private knowing, to love him. That bond, I knew, would not easily be broken.

And then the twins. Two tiny babies. Two little boys. But it was much easier the second time. Not only was I more prepared physically and emotionally, but I had also learned so much about the tender mercies of our Lord. I knew I had nothing to fear from this experience. God would again prove Himself to be strong in my weakness. He would again bathe my loneliness with an awesome display of His presence. He would again use my loss to open my eyes to all that I had in Him and in the blessings of my life.

At the time of my first miscarriage, I had been visiting my parents in Michigan. Because my husband was at our home in Illinois and had to drive several hours to reach the hospital, I was alone during most of the night—waiting for morning when the doctors would induce labor. I was feverish and for some reason the sedatives were ineffective. Though for some people sleeplessness at such a time would have been a curse, for me it was a tremendous blessing.

As I lay there alone in the darkness, I was overwhelmed by a sense of peace. I knew—not only intellectually, but also emotionally—that I had not been abandoned by the Lord. I was not at the mercy of nature or doctors. God was ultimately in control, and I was securely sheltered in the refuge of His divine presence.

That night, and in the quiet evenings which followed, I learned much about our refuge God, and about the comfort He offers us in times of need. I learned first that His is a *listening* comfort. With even the closest and most sympathetic of earthly friends, our communication is bound by the limits of words. But with Jesus, our communion knows no such limits. He can "listen" to the deepest cries and unspoken yearnings of our hearts. Without having to force our thoughts and feelings into inadequate words, we can have the assurance that they have been accurately heard.

I later learned that God offers us an *understanding* comfort. I was bothered that no one seemed to understand how I felt about that baby. A human life had come and gone and no one seemed to care! A person had existed and no one had even known it but me! Then I realized that Jesus, the great lover of the "little ones," understood exactly how I felt. He loved that baby too—and He knew it more perfectly than I did. It was, after all, His creation.

I learned too that our God offers us a *sensitive* comfort. He gave His presence, His empathy, and His ultimately comforting "I'm sorry" when that was just what I needed.

Some people tried to minimize the situation. "Miscarriages are common," they would say. Some even quoted the statistics of how many women have miscarriages. But I didn't care about that. When it happened to me, it hurt! It didn't devastate me, or cause me to shake my fist at God in anger. But it did make me feel very sad. And God responded to that sadness by covering me with the protective warmth of His love.

Help in Trouble

"God is our refuge and strength, a very present help in trouble" (Ps. 46:1). David was well aware of the "awesomeness" of His God. He was indeed humble before his God of power and perfection. He also knew, however, that this mighty transcendent God was his only hope, his only refuge against an evil world.

Refuge is a word that soothes the hearts of the needy. Those who have been bombarded by the pushes and tugs of a busy society seek the tranquility of a quiet place to hide—a refuge. Those who know the pain of grief seek a kind word and a loving arm to comfort them—a refuge. Those who know the disappointment of failure need someone to accept them as they are, to shelter them from the cries of a mocking world—a refuge. Those who know the tortures of temptation need a strong arm of righteousness to protect them from the lure of sin—a refuge.

Whatever our heart's cry, we need a refuge to run to—where we can be hidden, comforted, sheltered, and protected. David wrote many of his psalms during his fugitive years. Pursued by his enemy Saul, he knew well the need for protection and security. Night after night as he traveled through the mountainous countryside, he sought the shelter of a cave where he would be protected from an armed attack.

But David knew that such a refuge was imperfect and temporary. He knew that only in God would he find the ultimate refuge. Why? Because only in God rests the promise of omnipotence. A refuge that has no power offers no security. But a refuge that has all power offers ultimate security.

The psalmist said, "For Thou hast been a refuge for me, a tower of strength against the enemy" (61:3). That's exactly what we need—a tower of strength. And that's what we find in the Lord.

Charles Spurgeon said, "Where He is all power is, and all love, why therefore should we quail?" (*The Treasury of David,* Volume 1, Zondervan Publishing Co., p. 340) In that short sentence, he expressed the unique and overwhelming beauty of our refuge. It is a refuge built upon the dual foundation of God's unchallenged power and His everlasting love. In times of need, we can run to our place of refuge, assured that God's power will give us the strength we need, and His love will give us the comfort and encouragement we need.

Imagine how lost, how fearful we would be if our God displayed His power, but never in love offered His refuge. We would be alone in this universe, aware of the great power behind it, but never able to tap its source. But that is not how we stand in this world. We don't stand as lonely wanderers pitted powerlessly against our enemies. We are the children of the holy, almighty, transcendent God who has chosen to be our refuge—our protector.

In God's divine protection, we can be strong because He is our strength, safe because He is our shelter, and calm because our soul has found its rest in Him.

The Great Paradox

"How great is Thy goodness, which Thou hast stored up for those who fear Thee, which Thou has wrought for those who take refuge in Thee, before the sons of men!" (Ps. 31:19) Were God not good, He would be the ultimate ogre of the universe; but in His *goodness* He is man's ultimate friend. He is kind, tenderhearted, sympathetic, and full of goodwill. And fortunately for us, the outpouring of His goodness is dependent not upon the merit of the recipient, but simply on the goodness of His own divine nature.

Repeatedly throughout the Old and New Testaments, we read illustrations of God's goodness toward those who fear Him. His goodness would provide no comfort, however, were it not for His *faithfulness.* "Faithful is He who calls you," wrote Paul to the Thessalonians (1 Thes. 5:24). David too knew that this was true. God made promises to His children and He honored them. He responded to them as He said He would. Again and again, David claimed the promises of God, knowing God would stand behind them.

David's God was also the God of *mercy.* The Book of Psalms is a beautiful record of gratitude for this attribute of God. Mercy is God confronting human suffering and guilt with overflowing love and tenderness. A. W. Tozer calls it "a boundless, overwhelming immensity of divine pity and compassion" (*The Knowledge of the Holy,* Harper and Row, p. 97). It is extended to all creation, but none know it like believers, for through God's mercy we escape the punishment for our sins that we deserve.

Not only mercy, but also *grace* characterizes God's dealings with sinful men. Because of God's mercy, we *don't* get the punishment that we *do* deserve. Because of His grace, we *do* get the *blessings* that we *don't* deserve. We receive a salvation we don't deserve, a calling (as children of God) we don't deserve, and a destiny (heaven) we don't deserve. Grace is God imputing merit where none previously existed, and bestowing benefits on the undeserving.

David's God was also patient. Nothing is more evident in the history of God's people than the *patience* of God. His desire was not to judge them, but to bless them; so time and time again He left their wickedness unpunished as He waited for a sign of their heartfelt repentance. Because God is just, He must punish sinners, but not until He has exercised every ounce of His divine patience.

"I have loved you with an everlasting love," said the Lord to Israel through the Prophet Jeremiah (Jer. 31:3). In that statement He touched upon the most incredible aspect of His relationship with man. It is a relationship of *love*. God voluntarily became emotionally involved with His creation and identified with men. He took pleasure in His creation and concerned Himself with our welfare. To spare us the wrath demanded by His justice, He provided us a way of escape, through faith. He redeemed us. He loves us with a mighty love that has no beginning and no end—a love that is infinite, eternal, and unchanging.

That is the God of whom David said, "I love Thee, O Lord, my strength. The Lord is my rock and my fortress and my deliverer, my God, my rock, in whom I take refuge; my shield and the horn of my salvation, my stronghold. The Lord is my light and my salvation; whom shall I fear? The Lord is the defense of my life; whom shall I dread?" (Pss. 18:1-2; 27:1)

The fearsome God of majesty has become the protector who casts out our fear. The righteous Judge has become the source of our salvation. The mighty God before whom we tremble has become our refuge. And in that paradox we find the great beauty of our God.

If our God were just the God of majesty and power, we would surely fall on our faces and tremble before Him. We would fear Him with a holy fear and realize our need to submit to Him. But would we love Him?

If He were just the God of mercy and grace and compassion, we would surely love Him. But would we bow in awe before Him?

The glory of our God is that He is both of these. He is the Incomprehensible, the Holy, the High, the Mighty, and the Exalted. But He also chooses to be the ultimate lover of our souls, our best Friend. He is the Creator, the God of all the universe, yet He is the loving Father who calls us by name. A God like that we can worship in fullness. We can exalt Him. We can adore Him. We can submit our lives to Him. He is absolutely and unquestionably worthy.

Many Christians err by focusing solely on our "aweful" God, while others err by focusing solely on our "refuge" God. Those who see God only as the righteous judge live in fear, never certain of His forgiveness, acceptance, and love. Those who see God only as patient and loving are tempted to disobey Him and live carelessly. "God will forgive me," they flippantly say.

Both of these extremes are unhealthy. The attributes of God should not be held in contrast, but rather viewed together to provide a healthy concept of God. We ought to be so in love with the God of kindness that we are eager to please the God of righteousness. We ought to be so convinced of God's wisdom and His love that we can easily accept His will for our lives and walk in careful obedience.

The Boldness of Humility

After studying God's attributes discussed in this chapter, it is much easier for me to understand how David could approach the Lord so boldly. The awesome God is also the refuge God—the loving Father who gives His children unlimited access to His presence.

However, to grasp the significance of David's confidence before God, we must understand the nature of boldness itself. While there is a form of boldness rooted in man's pride, there is another form of boldness that finds its source not in man's pride, but in his humility—and that is the kind of boldness we find in David.

David said, "Give ear to my words, O Lord" (Ps. 5:1). At first glance, this appears to be a rather arrogant way to approach the holy God. We would expect something more like this: "Please, Lord, I know You don't have much time, but I'd really appreciate it if You would take a few moments to listen to me." Instead, David's plea sounds almost like a command.

In the next few words, however, we see the reason for David's firm appeal. "Give ear to my words, O Lord, consider my groaning. *Heed the sound of my cry for help,* my King and my God, for to Thee do I pray" (vv. 1-2). David was bold, but He was not bold in declaring his worth, as a proud man would be. He was, on the contrary, bold in declaring his need. His were the words of a humble man. The proud man doesn't ask for help, but the needy man asks without shame. And he asks in boldness, not because he deserves the help, but because he *needs* it so badly.

I have learned much from David in this regard. I should never hesitate to boldly declare my need to God. I should never hesitate to boldly ask for God's help or guidance. For in doing so, I admit my weakness and cast myself on His strength. I admit that I am merely the creature, while he is the Creator. And to such an attitude God responds with grace and help. He will always be a refuge for the needy.

A.W. Tozer said,

> Christ walked with men on earth that He might show them what God is like and make known the true nature of God to a race that had wrong ideas about Him. This was only one of the things He did while here in the flesh, but this He did with beautiful perfection.
>
> From Him we learn how God acts toward people. The hypocritical, the basically insincere, will find Him cold and aloof, as they once found Jesus; but the penitent will find Him merciful; the self-condemned will find Him generous and kind. To the frightened He is friendly, to the poor in spirit He is forgiving, to the ignorant, considerate; to the weak, gentle; to the stranger, hospitable.
>
> By our own attitudes we may determine our reception by Him. Though the kindness of God is an infinite, overflowing fountain of cordiality, God will not force His attention upon us. If we would be welcomed as the Prodigal was, we must come as the Prodigal came; and when we so come, even though the Pharisees and the legalists sulk without, there will be a feast of welcome within, and music and dancing as the Father takes His child again to His heart.
>
> The greatness of God rouses fear within us, but His goodness encourages us not to be afraid of Him. To fear and not be afraid— that is the paradox of faith (*The Knowledge of the Holy,* p. 90).

I know that one day I will see God as He really is and I will realize that there is only one appropriate response that I can make: worship. And I will probably regret the fact that I was not, during this lifetime, a more devoted worshiper. That thought challenges me. It motivates me.

I don't want to wait until I get to heaven to be a worshiper. God deserves my worship *now*. And I am committed to deepening my knowledge of Him so that I can become a better worshiper.

I don't think there is a higher goal than that.

5
Confession, the Inevitable Companion

"I never realized my ugliness till now. When I compare myself with you, I pity myself indeed, poor unhappy monster that I am! I must seem to you like some awful beast, eh? You—you are a sunbeam, a drop of dew, a bird's song! As for me, I am something frightful, neither man nor beast—a nondescript object, more hard, shapeless, and more trodden under foot than a pebble!" (*The Works of Victor Hugo,* Walter J. Black, Inc., p. 302)

With these plaintive words, Quasimodo, the notorious hunchback of Notre Dame, unveiled his soul to the beautiful gypsy girl, Esmeralda. Since his birth, Quasimodo had been haunted by the cruel specter of his deformity, but only when he stood in the presence of unmarred beauty did he see the full measure of his ugliness. In the light of Esmeralda's beauty, he saw new aspects of his deformity—hideous and grotesque disfigurations that he had previously overlooked—and he despised them because they rendered him unacceptable to her.

The worshiping Christian who stands in the presence of our holy God is like Quasimodo in the presence of Esmeralda. In the blazing light of God's beauty and holiness, we finally see our sin for what it is.

As a young child, I was rightly taught that I was a sinner who needed a Saviour, but seldom was I led to heartfelt remorse

53

because of my sin. Growing up in a Christian home, without ever expressing overt rebellion against my family or the Lord, I failed to develop a keen awareness of my sin. In terms of the external standards of Christian living I did very well, and it was remarkably easy to ignore the reality of my internal sin.

During the last year, however, as I have focused my attention on the God revealed in Scripture and have devoted myself to worshiping Him, I have had to join Quasimodo in facing up to who I really am. I have had to acknowledge the sin that I had previously ignored. In the presence of God, an acceptable exterior of mediocre Christian living just doesn't measure up. I have had to openly admit the impurity of my motives, the selfishness of my desires, and the frequent maliciousness of my thoughts.

This uncomfortable realization of my sin has, of course, left me with only one acceptable recourse: confession. When you're standing in the presence of a holy God and suddenly see that you are a dreadful sinner, there is only one reasonable thing to do— humble yourself, confess your sin, and ask for forgiveness.

Unfortunately, however, most of us would rather opt for the cover-up than the confession. We hate to admit that we've been wrong, or that we've violated another's rights. Of all the feelings that a human being can experience, guilt is one of the worst. It leads to the loss of self-esteem, to feelings of shame and despair, to a sense of isolation and loneliness, and to the fear of punishment and abandonment. It's an ugly, haunting monster that eats away at the fragile fiber of peace that we so desperately cherish.

Up with Your Defenses
To protect ourselves from the deadly attack of guilt, we carefully construct around our minds an impenetrable shield of defense. We plot out a precise pattern of thought that prohibits us from acknowledging our sin and insulates us from the pain of guilt.

In his book *Guilt and Forgiveness,* William G. Justice lists 37 of these oft-used defense mechanisms. I confess that as I read through his list of common defenses, I felt uncomfortably at home with many of them. In this chapter I want to mention just a few.

Probably no defense mechanism is used more frequently than

projection. This method, in which we shift the blame to another individual, is as old as the Garden of Eden. When God confronted Adam with his disobedience in eating the forbidden fruit, Adam's response was immediate. "The woman whom Thou gavest to be with me, she gave me from the tree, and I ate" (Gen. 3:12). "It wasn't *my* fault," said Adam. "It was Eve. Blame *her.*" When God confronted Eve, she did the same thing. "Hey, it wasn't my fault. It was the serpent. *He* made me do it."

There's always someone at fault—but it's never us!

The employee who feels guilty about unethical practices says, "The boss made me do it." The unsuccessful dieter who feels guilty about his lack of control blames a spouse who prepares rich foods. A workaholic father who feels guilty about his frequent absence from home blames the poor economy. The teenage girl who feels guilt about her sexual sin blames her boyfriend. A student who fails to make the grade blames the "stupid teacher."

On and on it goes. But no matter how hard we try to shift the blame to someone else, in the final analysis we are all left with our smoldering guilt. Our impenetrable shield of defense proves to be remarkably ineffective. Why? Because the Holy Spirit "will convict the world concerning sin" (John 16:8), and there is no way to escape that probing spotlight that always finds its mark. We can never *successfully* shift the blame to someone else.

Another popular defense mechanism is *rationalization.* The human mind is incredibly adept at creating compelling justifications for sinful behavior. The simple clichés are well known. "Everybody's doing it." "Nobody got hurt." "One wrong deed deserves another." "I'm only going to do it this one time." "He had it coming to him." These simple justifications are so easy to use— and so tempting.

Just today I caught myself using this means to assuage my guilt. My sin was an attitude of irritation and impatience toward my children. Everything they did or said was met by a sigh of displeasure, a cross word, or a look of untempered anger. I was tired and crabby, and I wasn't afraid to show it.

You see, we are awaiting the completion of our new house and have just begun a month-long stay at the home of some friends who are on vacation. It is a lovely place, well suited to the needs of a young couple, but not well-equipped for a family of four, with all of our "junk."

Needless to say, this once lovely home is now a place of chaos. How I wish I could put the house and everything in it back in perfect order, but there is simply no place to put all our belongings.

The problem is that I *hate* clutter. I *crave* peace and quiet and tranquility. And if there is any area in which I lack flexibility, it is this. I get crazy in disorganized situations. I can't relax. I can't stand it!

To add to the difficulty, the house is not air-conditioned, and the temperature must be near 100°. Shauna starts second grade tomorrow and we had to search through four boxes to find her "first-day-of-school" dress. I did a much-needed load of laundry only to find that the dryer didn't work. And as Bill walked out the door to leave on a week-long speaking engagement, he reminded me that the garbage pickup was the following morning.

"I'd put it out now," he said sympathetically, "but you know the city ordinance—no garbage on the street before 7 P.M. Sorry."

Oh, well, I thought. *What's one more problem?* And with that, I told myself that I *deserved* to be in a bad mood. I went along my crabby way, impatiently rushing the kids off to bed, then plopped down in a cluttered chair to wallow in self-pity.

But in the quiet of the post-bedtime moments, the Holy Spirit did His convicting work. "Paul learned to be content in whatever circumstances he was in" (Phil. 4:11), the Spirit reminded me, "and so must you. There is no acceptable excuse for selfish, insensitive behavior." My careful justification collapsed in the face of spiritual conviction, and there I sat with my guilt. Rationalization reduces guilt pains temporarily, but deep down inside the Holy Spirit continues to convict, and there's still that unavoidable burden of guilt.

Another common defense is *comparison.* "If you think *I'm* impatient, you should see the lady across the street!" "Oh, I know my personal devotions aren't what they should be, but some of the women in the study group *never* open their Bibles!"

"Well, maybe I am a little heavy on the gas pedal, but there's always someone going faster than I am." How we enjoy seeing other people's sin when it makes us look good by comparison.

A more sophisticated form of defense is *suppression.* If we cannot live with the reality of our sin or our mistake, we will attempt to submerge or suppress it. Unfortunately, this takes an incredible amount of emotional energy and the attempted suppression is never complete. The conscious mind does not easily give up its hold on reality. Like beach balls playfully submerged by youthful swimmers, the supposedly suppressed guilt will keep popping up to float unrestrained on the surface of our minds.

This unsuccessful suppression often leads to the next defense mechanism: *distraction.* Keep the television on. Keep the car radio blaring. Go to movies, plays, and parties. Use tranquilizers to rush the onset of sleep. Fill your schedule. Keep your date book overloaded. Regularly increase the speed of the treadmill, so that all you need to think about is the immediate. At all costs avoid the contemplation of the ultimate. Don't think. Don't meditate. Don't let your heart or mind be reminded of your guilt.

Closely related to distraction is *isolation.* Avoid the people and places that call you to accountability. Stay away from godly friends. Shun those who challenge you. Follow the example of Adam and Eve, who after they sinned, tried to hide in the bushes. They wanted to be alone. They wanted to avoid the convicting gaze of the holy God.

Finally, there is *escapism,* the all-time favorite for those who seek instant euphoria in a pill, a drink, or a fix. While most Christians avoid such obvious escapes, they seek the same end when they put more and more money into the offering plate instead of confessing sin, or when they pray as a substitute for taking action. No more guilt, no more pain, no more frustration— at least for awhile. But when the dulling drug wears off, when the dust settles, the insistent, internal, uneasiness of guilt remains.

A Real Life Example
If we're honest, we all have to admit that occasionally we indulge in a carefully planned game of defense. Deep inside we *know* our

sin, but we're not willing to acknowledge it.

David was no different from us in this regard. After committing adultery with Bathsheba, which led to consciously planned deception and murder, David began a period of "defensive living" that was broken only when he was directly confronted by the Prophet Nathan (2 Sam. 12:1-13).

We don't know what specific defense mechanism David used. Perhaps he used a combination. Maybe he blamed Bathsheba for his fall. After all, if *she* hadn't been bathing in such a visible place, he wouldn't have been tempted in the first place. Or maybe he rationalized his sin by citing his heavy burden of responsibilities— the administrative duties, the financial woes, the devastating effects of ongoing wars. Surely, if anyone had the right to indulge in a little extracurricular activity, it was David.

Perhaps David compared himself with pagan kings, and reasoned that his little misdemeanor was nothing compared with the immorality that ran rampant in their courts. Or maybe he tried to suppress his guilt, or distract himself by getting involved in the concerns of the kingdom.

Undoubtedly, David isolated himself from those who could have challenged him. He probably avoided the temple, and we certainly don't see him knocking on Nathan's door. He may even have given himself over to more than his usual consumption of wine.

But was David's defense successful? "When I kept silent about my sin, my body wasted away through my groaning all day long. For day and night Thy hand was heavy upon me; my vitality was drained away as with the fever heat of summer" (Ps. 32:3-4). These are not the words of one who has successfully escaped the clutches of guilt, but of one whose spirit has been ruthlessly crushed by it. Unconfessed sin in the heart of a believer is an inevitable source of frustration and despair, for guilt and peace of mind cannot coexist in the life of one who knows God. David learned that, and so have I.

But David also learned that the anguish of guilt can give way to the joy of forgiveness if we humble ourselves in confession. "I acknowledged my sin to Thee, and my iniquity I did not hide;

I said, 'I will confess my transgressions to the Lord'; and Thou didst forgive the guilt of my sin" (v. 5). David confessed and God forgave. In the end, David was able to say, "How blessed is he whose transgression is forgiven, whose sin is covered!" (v. 1)

A Model of Confession

The key to freedom from guilt is not found in a carefully planned defense system, but in sincere, honest confession.

But what exactly is confession? How do we begin? For those of us who are more adept at ignoring our sin than exposing it, where do we start?

I turned once again to the psalms for an answer. A friend of mine had just memorized Psalm 51 as a means of aiding her confessional life and I decided to do the same. I began reading the psalm over and over again each day, slowly memorizing it, using it as a pattern for my own prayers of confession.

Psalm 51 gives us a model of sincere confession and also a verbal picture of the heart of David as he confessed his sin before God. This picture is valuable not just because it aids our understanding of David, but because it shows us the kind of heart that we too should have when we approach the Lord. This psalm highlights the three progressions in David's confession: contrition, acknowledgment, and faith.

Contrition

"Be gracious to me, O God, according to Thy loving-kindness; according to the greatness of Thy compassion blot out my transgressions" (Ps. 51:1). So begins David's prayer. In David's request for forgiveness and cleansing, he appeals not to his own worth or merit, as one who deserves to be forgiven. Instead, he appeals to God's grace, loving-kindness, and compassion.

The unchanging attributes of God provide the only basis on which we can ask for forgiveness. Our God is gracious to sinners. He is compassionate to the brokenhearted. His loving-kindness is directed toward the repentant heart. His eternal, unchanging, loving nature is our only hope.

To learn this fact is to learn one of the great truths of the

Christian faith. We are, at all times, totally at God's mercy. We have no merit with which to earn His favor. We have no wealth with which to buy His blessing. Our only recourse is to appeal to His unchanging loving-kindness toward broken sinners.

The confessing heart, then, must be a heart cast upon God's loving-kindness. It must also be a heart that is grieved by its sinful ways. "For I know my transgressions, and my sin is ever before me" (v. 3). David is consumed with the horror of his sin. It haunts him. It grips him. He can't escape it.

Later he says, "Make me to hear joy and gladness, let the bones which Thou hast broken rejoice" (v. 8). In the anguish of his guilt, David knows no joy, no gladness. "Against Thee, Thee only, I have sinned, and done what is evil in Thy sight" (v. 4). David knew that his sin was done, in all its filthiness, right in front of the eyes of God. And that knowledge destroyed him. I can visualize David sitting with shoulders bent, head held in tired hands, wishing that he could blot the memory of his sin from his mind—and from God's. But he can't.

David's confession was a far cry from the flippant prayers read from denominational prayer books or whispered quickly by thoughtless Christians who have not yet come to grips with their own sin. It was the confession of a crushed heart, the kind of heart with which God is pleased—not because He delights in pain or destruction, but because He knows that it is only the truly broken heart that yields itself to forgiveness, cleansing, and healing.

I have committed neither adultery nor murder, but that surely makes me no less a sinner than David. At times, I have knowingly refused to meet my husband's needs; I have selfishly placed my own desires above the demands of my family; I have wounded my children with my words; and I have hurt my best friends with my insensitivity. David's prayer *is* my prayer. I have sinned in the sight of a holy God, and I need to come before Him with a broken heart.

Acknowledgment

In David's psalm of confession, we also learn of our need to be honest and open in acknowledging our sin. In contrition, we convey our heartfelt grief and our need to rest in God's loving-kindness. In acknowledgment, we give verbal confession to our specific sin. There is no room for projection, rationalization, comparison, or any of the other defense mechanisms.

How hard it is to say, "*I* am the guilty party. *I* did it. *I* am to blame." Just today I walked into a drugstore to buy some makeup and ran face-to-face into that ugly fact.

Up and down the aisles I went, searching for just the right item. Sometimes samples are provided, but never for the items of interest to me. Today was no exception. The cream-on blush in the tiny glass jars was altogether "sampleless."

The color I selected looked good in the jar, but how would it look on *my* skin? I knew that the unwritten rule of the cosmetics department was that jars should never, under any circumstances, be opened—but would one little dab hurt anything?

I removed the lid, gently touched my finger to the inside cover and smoothed a bit of the luscious color onto my hand. Hurriedly, I replaced the cover and slid the jar back into place—just as the sales clerk came to offer her unwelcome assistance.

"I'm sorry," she said, "we don't like to have our customers open the containers."

Guilty! I thought. *I was wrong. I owe this woman an apology.* But I couldn't make the words come out! I *knew* I was wrong. And I knew *she* knew I was wrong. But I still couldn't say it. Instead, I mumbled something totally unintelligible about samples and creams and powders, and asked her a question about something totally unrelated to what I needed. *Anything* to change the subject—to avoid the issue.

A few moments later I left the store, walked out to the car, and thought, *I can't believe I did that. First I knowingly disobeyed the rules of the store. Then I tried to avoid the truth about what I had done.* By the time I got home, I knew that I would have to return to that store and make my confession. If I didn't, I would be burdened by this nagging sense of guilt; I would alienate myself from the clerk in the store (I could visualize myself hiding behind display cases everytime I went there); and I would displease God.

Some people might think that this example is insignificant, that there is no cause to confess to the clerk. But to me it is far from insignificant, for it illustrates a very grave error on my part. I refused to acknowledge my wrongdoing. Oh, I didn't blatantly deny it. But I refused to be open and vulnerable. I refused to say, "I did it. I was wrong. I'm sorry." In that ordinary, commonplace incident, I glimpsed a side of myself that I don't like and I don't want to condone. My greatest desire is to be right with God—to be at peace with Him—and I can only do this if I willingly and readily acknowledge my sin.

Of course, I felt bad about what I had done in the store. If you had seen me there, you would have known that I was humbled. I was embarrassed. I was ashamed. I was contrite. But I wasn't willing to openly acknowledge my sin. And until there is acknowledgment, there can be no forgiveness.

This afternoon, on the way to the library, the kids and I made a quick stop at the drugstore. Unfortunately, the woman who had "caught" me had already gone home. I am sure, however, that she'll be there again tomorrow—and so will I.

Faith
"I have sinned," said David, and in so saying he modeled for us the only appropriate statement that we can offer God in regard to our sin. No excuses. No cover-ups. Just pure and unadulterated confession that springs from a broken and contrite heart.

But after we humbly cast ourselves on God's loving-kindness, openly acknowledge our sin, and ask for forgiveness, then what do we do? Do we wring our hands in despair? Do we anticipate a life of uneasy anxiety? Do we begin an unending pattern of self-condemnation?

God's Word says that if we confess our sins—come with a contrite heart and acknowledge our sin—God *will* forgive us (1 John 1:9). It doesn't say that He *might* forgive us. It doesn't say that if we happen to catch Him in a benevolent mood, He will turn the other way and ignore our sins. Rather, "He is faithful and righteous to forgive us our sins and to cleanse us from all unrighteousness." He removes the stain of guilt. He makes us pure.

David prayed, "Purify me with hyssop, and *I shall be clean*;

wash me, and *I shall be whiter than snow*" (Ps. 51:7). There was no doubt in David's mind about God's willingness or His ability to forgive and cleanse him.

God is infinitely gracious and has the power to forgive us and cleanse us from any sin. We can be free from the crushing weight of guilt. We can throw off our unsettling sense of uncleanness. By God's grace He forgives us, and when He forgives us He also cleanses us. He purifies us. He makes us *totally acceptable* in His sight.

An Unbroken Circle

Confession is an inevitable and inextricable part of worship. We cannot speak of worship without speaking of confession. Whether we say that confession leads us into worship or worship leads us into confession, we must recognize that they are both parts of the same unbroken circle. A contrite, broken, confessing heart is the only heart that can truly worship God. Likewise, a sincere, worshiping heart will always be drawn to a point of submission and confession.

It may seem that memorizing the confessional prayer of David is but one more way to perpetuate the meaningless repetition of empty words that so often tries to pass for true prayer. But I have not found it to be so. In David's words, I have found a way to express the thoughts of my own mind and the feelings of my own heart. As I have read and reread this psalm, I have been chastened, challenged, encouraged, and educated. And repeatedly these words creep back into my mind as gentle reminders to confess my sins.

"Deliver me from bloodguiltiness, O God, Thou God of my salvation; *then my tongue will joyfully sing of Thy righteousness.* O Lord, open my lips, *that my mouth may declare Thy praise*" (Ps. 51:14-15). With these words, David gives his response to God's gracious forgiveness—a response of joy, gratitude, and of course, worship.

6
God, Our Creator

"Man is a created being, a derived and contingent self, who of himself possesses nothing but is dependent each moment for his existence upon the One who created him after His own likeness. The fact of God is necessary to the fact of man. Think God away and man has no ground of existence" (A. W. Tozer, *The Knowledge of the Holy,* Harper and Row, p. 35).

If ever there is a statement that summarizes the scope of man's dependence upon his Creator, that is it. Unfortunately, however, it is a statement that few accept. The majority of mankind has, in ignorance and rebellion, denied its dependence upon God.

Imagine a craftsman who in his most creative moment shapes a statue of exquisite beauty. It is so superb that he decides to make of it more than a statue, and breathes into it the breath of life. As he does so, he dreams of the relationship that He will have with his living handiwork, and of the many wonderful joys that he will pour into its life.

As the dull eyes begin to sparkle with the glow of health and happiness, the craftsman smiles in pleasure. But soon his smile becomes twisted with the agony of disappointment as he sees the wild look of rebellion that wells up in the eyes of his creation.

The sculpted creature opens its mouth and with vehemence profanes the name of its maker. "You are nothing to me!" he cries. "How dare you claim a hold on me! Why should I relate to you? Who are you, anyway?" And so the creature disdains the mind that thought of him, and spurns the hand that fashioned him, thinking to find his own, perfect path to life.

As I meditate on that fanciful description of man's rejection of God, I realize how many times I have similarly failed to acknowledge and appreciate my Creator. I have refused to submit to His authority. I have feared the plan He designed in love for me. I have failed to thank Him for His gifts—His blessings—to me. I have taken lightly my relationship with Him. I have even questioned His existence.

Oh how I want to be continually aware that I am utterly dependent on God's creative power. I did not bring myself into existence, nor do I have the slightest power over the next breath I take. Any claim that I make of self-sufficiency and independence is a false and ignorant claim. God is the independent Creator; I am totally dependent upon Him.

A Reflection of Truth

Just as focusing on God's creative role has affected my attitude toward Him, so it has affected my attitude toward the natural order. No longer is nature *just* nature. It has suddenly become a vivid expression of God's creative impulse, and as Paul said, a reflection of "His invisible attributes, His eternal power, and divine nature" (Rom. 1:20).

In the rest of this chapter, let's examine nature as it offers to us a glimpse of God's wondrous glory and His awesome power, and as it graphically illustrates for us important lessons of spiritual truth.

A Glimpse of Glory

Dan DeHaan says, "God's creation is the greatest visible display of His glory. It is a foretaste on earth of what will come later" (*The God You Can Know,* Moody Press, p. 26). The psalmist too says, "The heavens are telling the glory of God" (Ps. 19:1), and Isaiah echoes that theme when he tells us that "the whole earth is full of His glory" (Isa. 6:3). Obviously, the beauty of creation is designed to give us a glimpse of God's glory.

Webster's Dictionary defines glory as "praise, honor, or distinction, accorded by common consent; renown; brilliancy; splendor; celestial bliss; heaven." Such a definition seems, on the surface, to be clear and easy to comprehend. It seems to fit with the biblical use of the term *glory*.

But does it really helps us imagine "the *glory* of God" as we will one day see it? Certainly it doesn't. Nor does anything else. There is no information or creative insight that can free our finite minds to create an accurate picture of the glory of our infinite God. To assume that we have such insight would be dangerously arrogant. We dare not claim such power.

On the other hand, we should not ignore the glimpse of God's glory that He has, by His grace, given us. In the elements of His creation, God has made many clear statements about Himself. In nature we see, not God Himself, but visual "figures of speech" by which He describes His glory in terms that we can understand.

Permanently etched into my memory is the beauty of the sunsets we enjoyed during our Lake Michigan vacation. Every evening as the sun appeared to sink slowly into the distant edges of the lake, the vibrant colors of the sky were reflected across the shimmering swells of water. These were no typical sunsets. The splendor of the skyscape was mirrored in the silver water, and enhanced by the white sands of the empty beaches and the graceful flight of the gulls silhouetted against the fiery sky—a spectacular sight!

But to me, it was much more than that. It was a message that said, "This is what the glory of God is like. It defies description. It evokes wonder and silence. It captivates the hearts of men and women, young and old. It makes you sorry to see it leave and eager to see it return again. It so outshines the gaudy dazzle of human accomplishments that it leaves you humbled and awed."

For me, the glory of God is no longer a nebulous idea. It has taken on shape and meaning in the beauty of the sunset, in the majesty of purple mountains, in the power of thunder and lightning, and in the holy whiteness of snow as it blankets the earth. These elements show me what God is like. From them, I catch invaluable glimpses of His glory.

I recently saw a news report about some West Coast divers who risked serious danger to rescue a whale caught in a net. At first, I questioned the divers' common sense in risking their own lives for an animal. But as I listened further and watched the film clips of the rescue, I found myself thinking, *Well, of course, they should try to rescue that animal. Look at its awesome size and strength. Imagine its intelligence. What an amazing creature!*

I remember feeling a similar appreciation for a pretty bay quarter horse that I occasionally rode. One afternoon as we moved from the enclosed pasture to the open trails, she decided to enjoy fully the freedom of being outdoors. Up and down the hills she charged, her mane and tail flying and her muscular shoulders surging constantly forward. Though her gait was smooth and I knew I was secure in the saddle, I realized quickly that she was not at all under my control. She was flying free in the wind. I was awed by her beauty, her strength, her power, and her speed. She was magnificent!

How impressed I am by these creatures of God's world—and so many others like them. The frail butterfly, who at just the proper time emerges from his cocoon to sport the colors of the rainbow in intricate design. The giant grizzly, who sleeps the winter away until he smells the scent of a warm day. The lowly salamander, who has the enviable ability to grow a new tail or leg if an old one is lost. The wandering albatross, whose instinctive understanding of aerodynamics and variant windspeeds allows him to travel long distances despite the remarkable weakness of his wing muscles. The fascinating angelfish, who uses the brilliance of his colors to advertise possession of territory and to ward off intruders.

If I can be so awed by these creatures—fellows with me of the created order—what will it be like to see God? Only then will I know the full meaning of the word *beauty. Majesty. Splendor. Power. Brilliance. Magnificence.* All these words with which we describe the most revered and appreciated elements of the earthly order, will be given new meaning when we see the glory of the revealed God.

Proof of Power

"I have made the earth, the men and the beasts which are on the face of the earth by My great power and My outstretched arm, and I will give it to the one who is pleasing in My sight" (Jer. 27:5). In this declaration to the Prophet Jeremiah, God established two significant points. First, He identified His power as the spark that fueled the vast creative energies required to bring this world into being. Second, He asserted His sovereignty over all that He had created ("I will give it to whom I please").

Repeatedly in Scripture, God uses creations as proof of His power and sovereignty. It is in the Book of Job, however, that He gives His most dramatic and convincing statements. In this record of Job's suffering, God is confronted with Job's frustration and despair, and with his friends' simplistic and self-righteous answers to the problem of suffering and evil. Listening to their insensitive debate as long as He can, God finally silences them all, and speaks from the midst of a storm.

> Who is this that darkens counsel by words without knowledge? Now gird up your loins like a man, and I will ask you, and you instruct Me!
> Where were you when I laid the foundation of the earth! Tell Me, if you have understanding, who set its measurements, since you know? Or who stretched the line on it? On what were its bases sunk? Or who laid its cornerstone, when the morning stars sang together, and all the sons of God shouted for joy? (Job 38:2-7)

Here speaks the Creator to the created. Here speaks the One who laid the foundations of the world to one who controls not even the strength of his own breath.

> Have you ever in your life commanded the morning, and caused the dawn to know its place? Have you entered into the springs of the sea? Or have you walked in the recesses of the deep? Have the gates of death been revealed to you? Or have you seen the gates of deep darkness? Have you understood the expanse of the earth? Tell Me, if you know all this.
> Have you entered the storehouses of the snow, or have you

seen the storehouses of the hail? Can you bind the chains of the Pleiades, or loose the cords of Orion? Can you lead forth a constellation in its season, and guide the Bear with her satellites? Do you know the ordinances of the heavens, or fix their rule over the earth?

Can you lift up your voice to the clouds, so that an abundance of water may cover you? Can you send forth lightnings that they may go and say to you, "Here we are?"

Do you give the horse his might? Do you clothe his neck with a mane? Is it by your understanding that the hawk soars, stretching his wings toward the south? Is it at your command that the eagle mounts up, and makes his nest on high? (Job 38:12, 16-18, 22, 31-33, 34-35; 39:19, 26-27)

Finally, God speaks to the heart of the issue. "Will the faultfinder contend with the Almighty?" He asks. "Let him who reproves God answer it" (40:2).

After hearing this great verbal display of God's creative power, Job gave the only appropriate response. He covered his mouth and stood in silent submission. No more did he contend with God. No longer did his carefully construed arguments seem worthy of debate. In the face of such awesome power and sovereignty, only one thing made sense: humble resignation and obedience.

"I know that Thou canst do all things, and that no purpose of Thine can be thwarted. . . . I have heard of Thee by the hearing of the ear; but now my eye sees Thee; therefore I retract, and I repent in dust and ashes," Job answered (42: 2, 5-6). By God's own admission, Job was the most godly man alive at that time (1:8). Yet when confronted with this graphic description of God's power, that godly man humbled himself in the most lowly form of repentance, and worshiped God.

What does this teach us about our response to the power of God displayed in His creation? Shouldn't we look at the dry leaves that dance and twirl in the twisting wind and worship the God in whose breath the wind finds its source? Shouldn't we quietly watch as darkness turns to dawn and praise the power that makes it so?

The psalmist said, "Let all the earth fear the Lord; let all the inhabitants of the world stand in awe of Him. *For He spoke and it was done; He commanded, and it stood fast*" (Ps. 33:8-9).

Personal Parables

On most mornings as I sit at this little glass-topped table and write, the brilliant morning sun filters through the lush green trees outside my window and fills the room with its warm glow. This morning, however, is different. A grey curtain of steady rain veils the stately trees, and the sky beyond them is dark. For the sunbathers and weekend vacationers, this rainy day is undoubtedly a grave disappointment. But to the dusty earth it is the gift of life.

As I watch the steady rain fall, I think of the dryness that occasionally settles in my own soul. The lack of vitality, the loss of joy, the inner weakness and emptiness. It is then that I must run to the place of refreshment—to the quiet presence of the Lord—where the rain of His life-giving Spirit can fall gently into my parched soul.

These words tell a truth which I have experienced time and time again. In the rush and pressure of life, it's so easy for me to drift slowly away from the source of my inner strength. As I meet the demands of people and responsibilities, giving from the limited supply of my own strength and love and patience, I become like the flower that has endured too long the burning effects of the sun. I need the life-giving arrival of a morning rain. I need the reaffirmation of God's unconditional love. I need to be made new, refreshed, strengthened. And God in His grace and mercy and patient loving-kindness does that for me.

I will never forget a certain early morning swim I enjoyed several years ago in the Tahquamenon River in upper Michigan. As I swam downstream with the sun at my back, I was amazed at the uninviting darkness of the water. How black it looked— how cold and mysterious. When I turned to swim back upstream, however, I swam into the most beautiful sea of silver that I had ever seen.

It was only when I swam into the sun that I saw the beauty of its light reflected on the waters. When I turned my back on it, I saw only darkness. I cannot think of that morning now without being reminded that each day I have the power to choose whether I will look toward the Son and enjoy the light of His presence, or turn away and be sucked into the darkness of sin.

Not all the lessons that nature teaches are quite so serious as that just mentioned. One time, during a brief walk through a local forest preserve, I stopped by a swampy little pond and sat under a leafless tree to enjoy the noisy antics of a lively bunch of geese. There are many strange sounds in nature, but few rival the loud honking of geese. As I sat there listening to their agitated banter, it suddenly hit me that our God must have a real sense of humor. Why else would He sprinkle this world with creatures that so readily draw out laughter from our hearts? Right there in that suburban forest preserve, I thanked God for His humor and I felt privileged to have gotten a glimpse into this facet of His divine character. Now, every time I see (and hear) a gaggle of geese fly overhead, I am gently moved to worship the God of glory and power—and fun!

Scripture Association

Another way to train ourselves to see God's lessons in His creation is to relate specific Scripture verses to the various elements of nature. For example, when you walk through the freshly fallen snow, think of Isaiah 1:18: " 'Come now, and let us reason together,' says the Lord, 'though your sins are as scarlet, they will be as white as snow; though they are red like crimson, they will be like wool.' " In the brief moments that it takes to recall and repeat that verse, you can think of God's forgiveness and offer Him the gift of your thanksgiving.

When you look up into a clear blue sky, think of Psalm 103:11. "For high as the heavens are above the earth, so great is His loving-kindness toward those who fear Him." Then worship Him for His loving-kindness. Never again will a blue sky be just a boundless expanse of empty space. It will be a personal message of God's love.

Or think of Isaiah 55:9. "For as the heavens are higher than the earth, so are My ways higher than your ways, and My thoughts than your thoughts." Look up into the sky and worship God for His matchless wisdom.

When you drive through the country and watch the wildflowers rush by your window, think of Matthew 6:28-30. "And why are you anxious about clothing? Observe how the lilies of the field grow; they do not toil nor do they spin, yet I say to you that even Solomon in all his glory did not clothe himself like one of these. But if God so arrays the grass of the field, which is alive today and tomorrow is thrown into the furnace, will He not much more do so for you, O men of little faith?" Thank God for His care and provision, and relinquish your anxiety over material needs.

When you wake up in the morning to the song of the birds, remember again what Matthew wrote. "Are not two sparrows sold for a cent? And yet not one of them will fall to the ground apart from your Father. But the very hairs of your head are all numbered. Therefore do not fear; you are of more value than many sparrows" (10:20-31). Thank God for His personal interest in you. If He is concerned about a tiny sparrow, how much more must He be concerned about the details of your life.

The little resort town which we frequently visit is the official "Blueberry Capital" of the Midwest. In a few weeks the many acres of carefully tended bushes will be covered with clusters of the bright blue berries. As in past years, I will cover the kids with mosquito repellent and head for the fields to fill our gallon buckets with the luscious fruit. As always, they will pop more berries into their mouths than into their buckets, but who cares? There will be berries in abundance!

And for me there will also be the constant reminder that only if I abide in Christ will I be able to "bear fruit" (John 15:4). As I walk up and down the rows of healthy, heavily laden bushes, I will be reminded that just as these branches remain strong and productive only as long as they are attached to the bush, so will I be strong and useful for my Lord only if I maintain a close and constant relationship with Him. Each dead branch that was torn away by the wind or pulled from the bush by a careless worker will warn me of the dangers of breaking my fellowship with my Lord. As I join the hundreds of other tourists who appreciate the visual beauty and delicious taste of this particular part of God's creation, I will also be drawn to worship the God from whom my strength comes—the God who is my "vine."

Nature is resplendent with symbolic reminders of great spiritual truths, and each of them is enough to bring a willing heart to worship. David said, "I will bless the Lord at *all times*; His praise shall *continually* be in my mouth" (Ps. 34:1). What better way to learn the art of continual worship than by enlisting the aid of these ever-present natural reminders?

There for the Seeking

I have always been a lover of nature. It seems apparent to the biased mind of this country girl that God did not intend for human beings to live in cities. Though my city-loving friends offer persuasive arguments to the contrary, my mind remains unchanged. I still prefer a leisurely stroll down a country road to a shopping trip in Chicago. I am much more impressed by the natural beauty of a common maple tree than I am by the architectural design of the Sears Tower. And I would rather wake up in the morning to the songs of the birds, than live in easy proximity to the more cultured sounds of the city.

I am not denying my appreciation for great art and music and architecture. Nor am I minimizing its value as a means of expressing true worship. But I am suggesting that in this busy, hectic world, it's easy to ignore the natural beauty that God created for us to enjoy.

There are many in Christian circles who deny the value of beauty in life. There are some who even consider it an evil. They value an object solely for its utilitarian dimension and look at the world through purely pragmatic eyes. But can we possibly be justified in looking at the world that way? Is that the way God sees it?

Last spring Bill and I and the kids spent a week in San Diego. One of the highlights of the week was our trip to the San Diego Zoo. Bill, with his fantastic memory, listened intently to all the facts and figures tossed out by the well-informed guide, and probably remembers them all to this day. But the kids and I were more concerned about picking our favorite animal attractions.

Todd liked the sea lions, Shauna fell in love with the koala bears, and I was absolutely fascinated by the exotic birds newly acquired from a renowned Chinese zoo. Housed in wire mesh cages, they were impossible to photograph, but in my mind I can see them yet. The brilliant hues, the dramatic plumes, the strangely shaped beaks, the intricate patterns created by the multicolored feathers. Were it not for the kids' wishes, I could have spent the entire afernoon soaking in the rare beauty of those amazing birds.

Several weeks later, I was similarly intrigued with the tropical fish at the Shedd Aquarium in Chicago. As I walked from window to window I was overwhelmed by the sheer number of species. I found myself thinking that God must have so enjoyed creating these little creatures that He forgot to stop! He kept adding new specimens with slight variations on old themes. Some looked so funny I couldn't help but laugh. Others were breathtakingly beautiful.

Always a lover of nature, I have now developed an intense appreciation for the One who created it. And that heightened enthusiasm for the Creator has enhanced my appreciation of His creation. It is one thing to look at a beautiful bird and appreciate it solely for itself. It is quite another thing to look at that same bird and realize that before it took on flesh and blood, it existed in the mind of God, that by His power it came into being, and that its exquisite beauty is a reflection of God's own perfect image.

Bill and I are committed to exposing our children not only to the wonders of man's technological and artistic achievements, but also to the beauty and power of God's creative handiwork. We want them to grow up with an awareness of God's creation that will instill in them an appreciation for His creative power and a knowledge of His multifaceted character.

What about you? What about your children?

Our world is a creative masterpiece of the living God. Will you open your eyes to its beauty, and your heart to its message?

7
God, Our Redeemer

About a year and a half ago, I noticed a lump on the right side of my neck. I watched it closely for several weeks and when it didn't go away, I decided to see a doctor. I wasn't extremely concerned about it until my doctor referred me to a specialist and insisted that I see him immediately. At that point, I began to wonder, *What if there is something seriously wrong with me? What if the doctor's report confirms the worst?*

On the way to the specialist's office, caught in late afternoon traffic, I asked myself, *What can I count on in this life? What do I have that can't be taken away?*

In one short week, I had come face-to-face with the fact that my good health could easily be snatched away. And what about my family? My love for them held no ultimate protective power. They could be taken away in an instant.

So too with my abilities, my goals, my earthly freedoms. On through the list I went, mentally checking off the things that were important to me. Each of them was vulnerable. Each could be destroyed or taken away. Even life itself held no guarantees.

This may sound like a morbid mind game to play on the way to a doctor's office. However, God used those few uninterrupted moments to lead me to this realization: If all that we value in this life—every earthly thing that we love and enjoy—were suddenly taken away, we would still have cause to rejoice. Why? Because we would still have the most valuable treasure that a human being can possess—the knowledge and promise of our salvation.

My visit to the specialist was uneventful. To him, it was obvious that the lump was merely fibrous tissue and nothing to worry about. He affirmed my robust health and sent me home.

I can still feel that lump on the side of my neck. Though no longer a source of concern, it serves as a constant reminder of that experience and the lesson I learned. We believers are the richest people around. We have in our possession the ultimate gift—the eternal, unchanging promise of salvation. No one can ever take that away from us.

The Source of Joy

In light of this truth, isn't it amazing how quickly we allow ourselves to be defeated and embittered by minor irritations and trivial problems? We get upset if the car doesn't start, or if we're passed up for a promotion at work. It's a major crisis if we find a grey hair. And if our plans are interrupted, we get angry and feel taken for granted. We focus on negatives and lose our perspective.

How foolish we are! We're like a man with a $10 million bank account who worries and complains because he misplaces a $20 bill. To that man we would say, "Hey, don't worry about the pocket change. Look at all you've got!"

Those of us who want to be true worshipers have to quit worrying about the pocket change too. We have to take our eyes off what we *don't* have, and start focusing on the wonderful things that we *do* have.

"But I have trusted in Thy loving-kindness," said David, "my heart shall rejoice in Thy salvation. I will sing to the Lord, because He has dealt bountifully with me" (Ps. 13:5-6). For many of us, rejoicing in our salvation takes discipline. Most of us are not naturally positive thinkers. We don't easily focus on all that is true and right and eternal and lovely. So we must consciously teach ourselves to appreciate our salvation. We have to learn to say, "I will not allow this problem or this irritation or this defeat to rob me of the joy of my salvation. I will meditate on all that God has done for me, and *I will be glad!*"

Paul tells us to "rejoice in the Lord always" (Phil. 4:4). He is not speaking of a superficial *Praise the Lord anyway!* attitude, but of a deep-seated contentment based on the understanding that our salvation is more important than anything else. It is worth far more than all the trifling incidentals that weave in and out of the fabric of our lives. It is the ultimate value.

If anyone allows matters of little consequence to rob them of their joy, it is me. How it must grieve the Lord to see a child of His, redeemed and adopted into His family, discouraged by minor problems or angered by petty irritations. As has happened so many times during the writing of this book, I sit at my typewriter again under conviction. I have for so long failed to appreciate my salvation and neglected to worship the Holy God of Israel as my Redeemer.

In the remainder of this chapter, let's focus on God's redemptive plan as revealed to His chosen people, Israel. Though a well-known story, none serves better to turn our hearts toward worship.

Precious Blood

"You were not redeemed with perishable things like silver or gold from your futile way of life inherited from your forefathers, but with precious blood, as of a lamb unblemished and spotless, the blood of Christ" (1 Peter 1:18-19). In God's economy, the violation of His holiness must be atoned for in blood. No payment of silver or gold, no matter how great its amount, can ever buy our redemption. Nothing but the shedding of blood can free us from the condemnation we deserve.

I have never understood why God insisted on the shedding of blood. It seems to me that He could have decided upon another equally effective means of atoning for sin. How much nicer it would be to talk of redemption in terms more sophisticated and philosophical. Like many other Christians, I would prefer to avoid the subject of blood. It seems so crude and violent.

But God, in His infinite wisdom, has ordained that only the

sacrifice of blood can vindicate His holiness. When we sin we violate the righteousness of God, and in so doing earn for ourselves the penalty of death. Justice demands that the penalty be paid and that the blood be shed—and there is no exception.

But the blood need not be ours. In His loving-kindness and grace, God has chosen to give us a way out, to free us from the penalty of death. He has provided a substitute—a Lamb unblemished and spotless—who died in our place.

That, in simple terms, is redemption. God does not wave a magic wand and erase the reality of our sin. Nor does He sidestep the demands of justice and waive the penalty that is due. God is just, and He cannot contradict His own character by ignoring the demands of justice. He can, however, arrange to have someone else meet those demands on our behalf. And that is exactly what He has done.

The Price is High

Imagine yourself in Eden. The fragrance of springtime blossoms awakens your senses to the dramatic display of life around you. You hear the mingled melodies of the birds that soar overhead. Your eyes scan slowly the pallet of color that encircles you. The unending blue of the sky. The vibrant green of the lush foliage. The rich reds and yellows and browns that define the birds and animals of the woodland. It is a glorious world of beauty and peace—and perfection.

But the perfection is not to last. In your desire to be like God, you eat of the forbidden fruit. Immediately your eyes are opened and you realize that you are naked—vulnerable and exposed. In desperation, you gather some fig leaves together, fashion them into a crude garment, and cover yourself.

You walk quietly through the many pathways, until suddenly you hear the sound of the Lord walking in the garden. Always before that was a welcome sound, but today it sparks a sense of dread—even panic. Running quickly but silently to the densest part of the garden, you hide among the trees. Lower and lower you crouch until your knees touch the brown earth.

"Where are you?" God asks. But surely He already knows. He

is the Master of the garden. He knows each path, each secret corner.

"I heard You in the garden, and I was afraid because I was naked; so I hid myself." Anxiously, you wait for God's response.

"Have you eaten from the forbidden tree?" He asks, and how can you deny your sin? You know that He knows all. You can't hide a thing from Him. In shame, you admit your sin and listen as the Holy One pronounces a curse upon you.

Then, you watch in horror as God slays an innocent animal and makes a garment of skins for you. Never before have you heard the cry of pain or seen the blood of death. Hesitantly, you throw aside the fig leaves and put on the new robe. *Why was the change necessary*, you wonder? *What was wrong with the fig leaves?*

You are afraid to express your questions, but God anticipates them. "I know you thought you could cover your own shame," He says, "but you can't. Only I can adequately cover your shame." (See Gen. 3:1-24.)

In this story from Scripture, we see a vague foreshadow of the redemptive plan that is revealed more clearly later in God's Word. Throughout the Old Testament this theme is repeated with ever-increasing clarity until we find its full revelation in the Gospels.

The Passover

We see a major step in this progressive revelation in the Book of Exodus, which tells of Moses' attempt to lead the Children of Israel out of Egypt. God has sent nine plagues as a means of persuading Pharaoh to allow the Israelites to leave, but still his heart remains hard (Ex. 7:14—10:27). Pharaoh refuses to sanction their exit. So God decides to send one final plague.

"About midnight," He says, "I am going out into the midst of Egypt, and all the firstborn in the land of Egypt shall die, from the firstborn of the Pharaoh who sits on his throne, even to the firstborn of the slave girl who is behind the millstones; all the firstborn of the cattle as well" (11:4-5). No Egyptian household will be spared the grief and agony of death.

But for the Children of Israel, God provides a plan of protection. He commands the head of each household to kill an unblemished male lamb and sprinkle the blood on the two doorposts of his house. Then the family is to eat the lamb with unleavened bread and bitter herbs (12:3-8).

God tells Moses the reason for the slaying of the lamb and the sprinkling of the blood:

> For I will go through the land of Egypt on that night, and will strike down all the firstborn in the land of Egypt, both man and beast; and against all the gods of Egypt I will execute judgments—I am the Lord. And the blood shall be a sign for you on the houses where you live; and when I see the blood I will pass over you, and no plague will befall you to destroy you when I strike the land of Egypt (vv. 12-13).

At midnight, God carries out His judgment:

> And Pharaoh arose in the night, he and all his servants and all the Egyptians; and there was a great cry in Egypt, for there was no home where there was not someone dead. Then he called for Moses and Aaron at night and said, "Rise up, get out from among my people, both you and the sons of Israel; and go, worship the Lord, as you have said. Take both your flocks and your herds, as you have said, and go, and bless me also" (vv. 30-32).

Where there was no blood, there was death and destruction. But where the blood was, there was absolute protection. As a result of God's protective care, the Israelites were spared judgment, and were released from Egypt.

The Ultimate Sacrifice
Innocent blood was also shed repeatedly in the burnt offerings of the Old Testament. Again and again we see the same theme. Man stands as a sinner before God, deserving the death that would meet the demands of God's justice; but by grace God frees man from condemnation and provides an acceptable substitute to die in his place.

This basic theme was illustrated repeatedly by Old Testament worshipers, but still man's understanding of the concept was fuzzy. Revelation had not yet progressed to the point where godly men could anticipate the ultimate and final Sacrifice.

In Isaiah 53, however, revelation takes a quantum leap. The sacrifice is no longer described as *it,* the lamb—but rather as *He,* the Man:

> But He was pierced through for our transgressions, He was crushed for our iniquities; the chastening for our well-being fell upon Him, and by His scourging we are healed. All of us like sheep have gone astray, each of us has turned to his own way; but the Lord has caused the iniquity of us all to fall on Him. He was oppressed and He was afflicted, yet He did not open His mouth; like a lamb that is led to slaughter, and like a sheep that is silent before its shearers, so He did not open His mouth (Isa. 53:5-7).

Here we are given a revelation that makes the pathos of the unblemished lamb seem paltry and inconsequential. One day the ultimate Sacrifice would be offered, and it would be no mere dove or pigeon or goat or lamb. It would be a perfect Man, "pierced through for our transgressions," and "crushed for our iniquities." An innocent Man who would shed His blood for the sake of the guilty.

The Completed Plan

With this in mind, it is with new understanding that we read the words with which John the Baptist identified Jesus. "Behold, the Lamb of God who takes away the sin of the world!" (John 1:29) In those few words, John the Baptist placed the finishing touches on the progressive revelation that had begun centuries before. In his recognition of Jesus, he announced the arrival of the human Lamb—the ultimate and final Sacrifice.

The Jews should have known at that moment that innocent blood would be shed. Jesus knew it. Throughout His ministry He proclaimed His purpose and His destiny. "The Son of man did not come to be served, but to serve, and to give His life a ransom for many" (Matt. 20:28). "And as Moses lifted up the serpent in the wilderness, even so must the Son of man be lifted up; that whoever believes may in Him have eternal life" (John 3:14-15). "I am the Good Shepherd; the Good Shepherd lays down His life for the sheep" (John 10:11). On and on He taught until the day the prophecy came to complete fulfillment.

In the Garden of Gethsemane, the innocent Lamb of God was betrayed. He was arrested. He was forsaken by all. And when He was tried as a criminal, He said nothing in protest. He was beaten with rods and flogged and whipped and spit upon. His beard was plucked. Finally, the innocent, unblemished Lamb was stripped and pounded to a wooden cross where His blood flowed freely. Ridiculed and shamed, He died a slow and excruciating death. (See Matt. 26:36-56; 27:30-31; Mark 15:5; Luke 23:26-46.)

Imagine the horror in heaven as the innocent Son shed His blood for the guilty and rebellious inhabitants of Earth. The angels watched, along with the saints. "Unfair, unfair, unfair!" they wanted to scream, and in their hearts they echoed the cries of the few scattered followers who huddled in horror at the foot of the cross. *Why did He have to die?* they cried. *What did He do?*

The answer is simple. In God's economy, there is no forgiveness without the shedding of innocent blood.

Paul writes, "Christ our Passover also has been sacrificed" (1 Cor. 5:7). What was the purpose of the blood of the Passover lamb? To protect the Israelites from God's inevitable judgment. That is exactly what the shed blood of Christ does for us. He is, in every sense, our Passover Lamb.

When we stand in judgment before God, we will not be asked about our moral standing, our church attendance, or our giving patterns. We will answer just one question. *What did you do with the blood that was shed for you?* Did you apply it to the doorpost of your life? Did you rely on that ultimate sin offering as your only hope of cleansing? Or did you sew a few fig leaves together and try to cover up your shame and sin in your own way? Did you think, like Pharaoh, that you could stand against the destroyer on your own?

We cannot stand against the destroyer—or God's judgment—
anymore than Pharaoh could. Our only hope is to cling to the
sacrifice that was made for us by the Lamb of God. But what a
hope it is! It is a hope based on the guaranteed promises of an
unchanging Father.

We may doubt that the sun is going to rise in the morning or
that the moon will give its gentle light at night. But we can never
doubt that we are loved people. God established that point beyond dispute, and in that love we can bask and rest and rejoice.

When Paul and Silas sang praises in their filthy dungeon at
midnight, it was not because they enjoyed standing with hands
and feet in stocks, or because the beatings they had previously
endured had proven to be exhilarating (Acts 16:23-25). Rather,
in contemplating the love of God and the sacrifice of the Lamb,
they were irresistibly drawn to worship God and sing praises to
Him.

In the same way the early Christians sang songs of joy and
worship as they were thrown to lions, as they were burned at the
stake, as they were smothered in boiling pitch. They rejoiced not
in their circumstances, but in their Saviour. They sang praises
to the Lamb who was worthy. They were overwhelmed with the
joy of their salvation, even in the face of pain and persecution and
death.

It was over a year ago, at a Labor Day Leadership Retreat,
that Bill first presented the material that gave birth to this book.
Since then, as I have concentrated on worship and studied the
attributes and works of God, I have realized more and more how
much I have to be thankful for. My God has done such tremendous things for me!

Not long ago, I attended another Labor Day Leadership Retreat. There, as I thought over some of my past goals, I realized
that too often my goals had been stated in negative terms. "Quit
doing this. Overcome that. Break such and such habit." But this
year I decided upon a single goal which was simple and concise
and stated in a positive way. "Rejoice more!" My theme verse
is Philippians 4:4: "Rejoice in the Lord always; again I will say,
rejoice!"

I have no reason to be a joyless person. Regardless of what minor irritations or major traumas I may face, I have cause for rejoicing. I have in my possession the ultimate source of joy. I have the Lord—and He has loved me, called me by name, and redeemed me.

8
God, Our Sustainer

Pick Your Own Plum Tomatoes! read the sign on the roadside. *How interesting,* I thought, as I looked across the acres of carefully tended plants.

I focused my attention back on the road just in time to slam on the brakes. The driver ahead of me had stopped, waiting to make a left turn. I managed to avoid his rear bumper by inches.

"Thank You, Lord," I whispered. "How often You have rescued me."

Though it's not uncommon for people to say a flippant "Thank God" when potential harm is avoided, or to casually give God credit when good things happen, my whispered "Thank You" was neither flippant nor casual. It was my sincere acknowledgment of God's protective hand on my life.

God did not give me breath and then leave me to flounder through life on my own. No, He has guided and cared for me since the day I was born. Were it not for His constant protection and His loving care, I would long ago have been overcome by the potential dangers and temptations common to this world.

General Sustenance
When I was in college, I had a car that I thought was the ultimate in transportation. It was a blue, three-speed Firebird with a white

convertible top and white racing stripes. I loved it! It was quick and sporty and loud. It was not, however, too dependable under the hood.

I remember many times driving home on weekends thinking, *I hope this thing holds together till I get home.* And then I'd think the same thoughts on my way back to school. Of course, when I said "holds together," I wasn't really worried that the doors or the bumpers would fall off. I only hoped the car would keep running long enough to get me to my destination.

In Colossians we learn that in Christ "all things were created" and "all things *hold together*" (Col. 1:15-17). God, through Jesus Christ, not only created the world, but He also maintains and sustains it. He energizes it. He "keeps it running."

Imagine what would happen if God decided to withdraw His sustaining hand from the universe. The sun, moon, stars, and planets would all run wildly out of control. Weather patterns, temperatures, ocean currents, and gravity would all be affected. Life as we know it could not continue.

But how much credit has God been given for His sustaining work in this world? Until recently, I seldom thought about God's sustaining work in my own life, let alone His sustaining work in the world. I took the smooth functioning of the natural order for granted. And I think many others have shared my ingratitude.

Unfortunately, however, ingratitude is not our only sin. Just as we have failed to appreciate God's sustaining power, so we have failed to cooperate with it. We have stripped this world of its resources by endangering its species, burning its forests, paving its fields, and polluting its water and air. But still God sustains the marvels of nature.

Being an avid sailor, my husband recently attended a class on the art of celestial navigation. Before the development of electronic navigational equipment, all ocean navigation was based on the precise location of the sun, the moon, the stars, and the planets. Throughout most of the history of our world, sailors have accurately charted their courses across thousands of miles of open seas by relying solely on the ordered movements of the celestial bodies.

Not long ago a pilot who flies for a leading commercial airline revealed that occasionally on cross-country flights, when the airplane is set on auto-pilot and weather conditions are calm, he takes some form of celestial navigation and checks his own electronic navigation systems with the stars. "There's one thing we know," he said. "The stars are never wrong. Never!"

Yes, God has sustained the elements of nature with precision and care over thousands and thousands of years, yet seldom do we give Him the credit He deserves. We praise the accomplishments of technology and the skills of man, while forgetting to worship the God upon whose sustaining hand all human achievement is predicated.

Like us, the Prophet Habakkuk occasionally doubted God's involvement in the ongoing course of history—not in terms of nature, but in regard to society. He accused God of ignoring the evil plots of wicked men and closing His eyes to the plight of the people who were oppressed. God responded like this: "Look among the nations! Observe! Be astonished! Wonder! Because I am doing something in your days—you would not believe if you were told" (Hab. 1:5).

It's as if God were saying, "Wait a minute, Habakkuk. You don't have the whole picture. You think that I am not at work in this world, but I am. In fact, you wouldn't believe all the things that I'm doing behind-the-scenes."

God then explained to Habakkuk some of His plans for the future and assured him that He was in control. He was not out of touch with His creation. He was watching over it, ordering it, "holding it all together."

Personal Sustenance

It is not, however, just in the overseeing of nature and society that we see evidence of God's sustaining work. In our personal lives as well, we enjoy the benefits of divine concern. As our Creator, God awakened us to life in the flesh, and as our Redeemer, He awakened us to life in the Spirit. Now, as our Sustainer, He gives us all the resources we need to meet our material needs, our physical needs, and our spiritual needs.

Divine Provision

When Bill and several associates decided to leave the youth ministry they had been involved in and begin an adult ministry, they did so with the firm belief that theirs was a call from the Lord. So they began, with no people, no property, no assets, no experience, and certainly no guaranteed income.

As the plans for our "church" became more and more concrete, it also became more evident that there was no way to launch the dream except to go out on a limb—to throw ourselves wholeheartedly into the ministry and rely on God to meet our material needs. So we did it, and of course God was faithful. Whether He provided buyers for our unneeded possessions (so we could use the income for living expenses) or provided odd jobs that afforded just those few extra dollars we needed, He was faithful in sustaining us through some very lean years.

To a skeptical outsider, such "divine provision" may have appeared to be mere coincidence or "luck." But to those of us who knew the power of prayer and saw the quiet interplay of details that defied human reason, there was no doubt that we owed our gratitude to the sustaining hand of God.

> For this reason I say to you, do not be anxious for your life, as to what you shall eat; nor for your body, as to what you shall put on. For life is more than food, and the body than clothing. Consider the ravens, for they neither sow nor reap; and they have no storeroom nor barn; and yet God feeds them; how much more valuable you are than the birds!
>
> And which of you by being anxious can add a single cubit to his life's span? If then you cannot do even a very little thing, why are you anxious about other matters? Consider the lilies, how they grow; they neither toil nor spin; but I tell you, even Solomon in all his glory did not clothe himself like one of these. But if God so arrays the grass in the field, which is alive today and tomorrow is thrown into the furnace, how much more will He clothe you, O men of little faith!
>
> And do not seek what you shall eat, and what you shall drink, and do not keep worrying. For all these things the nations of the world eagerly seek; but your Father knows that you need these

things. But seek for His kingdom, and these things shall be added to you (Luke 12:22-31).

If we love and worship the Lord and strive to please Him, then we have no cause to worry about temporal needs. We may not know *how* God will take care of our needs, but we can be assured that He will. He may do so by providing a much needed job. Or by giving us the energy to work harder. He may give us insight into how we can minimize our material needs, how we can lower our standards. He may even send us someone who is willing to share his resources with us. We never know *how* God may choose to meet our material needs, but we can have confidence that He *will.*

Jody, Jack, and Jan

Just as God sustains us materially, so He sustains us physically. When I contemplate this truth, I think of my friend Jody, a lovely and godly lady who suffers from acute leukemia. Seven years ago her disease was diagnosed and she was given just a short time to live. Miraculously, however, she outlived the doctor's prediction, and she has since faced repeated crises which doctors considered hopeless, only to be once again strengthened and revived.

Jody is a beloved teacher in our church, and an example that has provided challenge and encouragement for hundreds of men and women, both young and old. Consequently, she has been the subject of thousands of prayers for healing, issued fervently on her behalf. She has also willingly accepted a wide variety of treatments, believing that God often chooses to send His healing power through the work of skilled physicians.

But the volume of prayers and the treatments have not led to Jody's healing. They have, however, led to a new appreciation for what it means to be sustained; though Jody has not been freed from her illness, she has been lovingly and gently upheld in the midst of it.

Time and time again she has been snatched from the claws of death, her body defying medical expectations. She has also been able to live day by day, through seven years of pain and human disappointment, with a deep, soul-stirring joy. How has she done it? By relying on the power of a gracious Father, who has sustained her frail body against all odds, and her gentle and joyful spirit even in the face of severe trial.

Jody's illness has brought many people in our church together in a close bond of prayer. Each new crisis has called forth another avalanche of prayer, and each miraculous answer has resulted in a fresh outpouring of praise. But Jody is not the only one for whom we've prayed and in whom we've seen evidence of God's sustaining power.

There's also Jack, the commercial airline pilot. Though he had attended another church regularly for years, he had never heard a clear presentation of the true Gospel. When he finally began attending our church and heard the biblical message of salvation, he responded by acknowledging Christ as His Lord and Saviour. Little more than a year later, he was stricken with cancer. Though mature in body and mind, Jack was still a spiritual baby. Faced with the trauma of such a dreaded disease, he had only one recourse—to avail himself of the support and encouragement offered by other Christians, and request their prayers for his growth, strength, and healing.

In the months and years that have followed, we have witnessed not only Jack's *physical* healing, but also the rapid growth of his *spiritual* understanding and sensitivity. Eager to share with others what God has done for him physically and spiritually, he has become a source of challenge and inspiration to many people.

Then there's Jan, a young girl who loved the Lord so much that her vibrancy and verbal witness sparked the flame of spiritual awakening in many others. When she was stricken, at age 20, with a very rare form of cancer, she began, along with other Christians, to pray earnestly for healing. But she also declared to the Lord that she would willingly love Him and serve Him with joy, whatever the outcome of her illness. Jan did just that—loved and served her Lord with joy—until her death at age 22.

When we prayed for Jody, the Lord answered by giving us clear evidence of His sustaining work in her life. When we prayed for Jack, the Lord answered by healing him. But what about Jan?

We prayed for her, and she died. We earnestly asked God to heal her as He did Jack, or at least to sustain her as He had done and continues to do for Jody. But He did neither. He let her die.

Did God fail Jan? What would *she* say? Those who knew Jan well claim that she had no complaint against God's work in her life. On her deathbed, she radiated the same joy and love for God that had characterized her entire life as a Christian. She sincerely believed that God *had* sustained her—even though He hadn't healed her or strengthened her body. He had strengthened her spirit, and what, she would ask, was more important than that? While others asked *why,* Jan never had to. She was perfectly content to leave this world, sustained by her love for God and her hope of heaven.

Water for Thirsty Souls

The God who procured our salvation will not leave us to flounder in the quagmire of spiritual confusion or immaturity. Just as He sustains us materially and physically, so He sustains us spiritually. He gives us all we need for growth and stability, and protects us from the forces of spiritual darkness so active in our world.

First, God sustains us by reaching out to us during times of spiritual drought. At some time, every Christian has experienced that frustrating feeling of spiritual emptiness and exhaustion. You feel like you're wandering in the wilderness, searching for the clear waters of spiritual refreshment, but finding only the bitter waters of stagnation. The joy of your salvation has given way to an oppressive awareness of failure and sin.

I have surely experienced those times; but I have also experienced the tender touch of the Sustainer, who reaches down to the driest, dustiest soul and opens anew the springs of living waters. "The Lord is my shepherd, I shall not want. He makes me lie down in green pastures; He leads me beside quiet waters. *He restores my soul"* (Ps. 23:1-3).

As I think back over the last few years, I can remember vividly the feelings of failure and dejection that have accompanied my spiritual droughts. I remember the nagging fear that I had finally drifted too far from the source of living waters, that there was no turning back, that the joy was gone forever. I remember that prayer was meaningless, Scripture said nothing, and the words of Christian friends sounded hollow and empty. And it didn't seem possible that this could ever change. My spiritual life seemed dead.

But of course that wasn't true. In desperation, I threw myself upon the mercies of God, and like the psalmist, I was refreshed—my soul was restored.

Sin and human weakness will continue from time to time to thwart the work of the Spirit in my life, and occasionally it will even cause my faith to waver and my spirit to drift alarmingly far from its source of power and joy. But sin can never *destroy* the life of my spirit, for always—repeatedly, again and again and again—God will respond to the cry of a sincere heart and will restore my soul.

No Temptation Too Great

Second, God sustains us spiritually by protecting us from the temptations of the evil one. Satan has no shortage of dirty tricks which He delights to play on believers. He loves to lay snares in our pathways. He wants us to act against our consciences and compromise our integrity, and he provides ample opportunities for us to do so.

But in each of these tempting situations, we have recourse to a sure means of escape. "No temptation has overtaken you but such as is common to man; and God is faithful, who will not allow you to be tempted beyond what you are able, but with the temptation will provide the way of escape also, that you may be able to endure it" (1 Cor. 10:13).

Temptation is an unavoidable reality of life. We cannot live above temptation. We are not, however, defenseless against it. We have a Protector, the Lord, who will keep us from being tempted in a way that we can't endure, and will also provide us with an alternative to sinful behavior.

Of course, we can spurn God's protection against temptation, and we've all done that at various times. We have ignored His alternative and yielded to sin. But as we grow in our Christian lives, we learn the value of grabbing hold of the alternative. God doesn't force His alternatives to sin on anybody, but they're always there if we're willing to reach out for them. If we do, we will overcome temptation, and we will soon learn to appreciate deeply the personal intervention of our holy God.

Never Abandoned

Third, God sustains us spiritually by giving us an added measure of grace during times of trial.

From time to time, it seems that the hand that holds back the reservoir of personal tragedies is lifted and we are swept away in a sea of trouble. Our hearts ache with grief as we suffer through the pain of illness or rejection or disappointment, or the loss of a loved one through death or divorce. We feel like children neglected by the mother who promised to love us, and abandoned by the father who promised to protect.

But have we really been neglected and abandoned? Are we orphans left to fend for ourselves in a hostile world? God says, "Do not fear, for I have redeemed you; I have called you by name; you are Mine! When you pass through the waters, I will be with you; and through the rivers, they will not overflow you. When you walk through the fire, you will not be scorched, nor will the flame burn you. . . . Since you are precious in My sight" (Isa. 43:1-2, 4).

These are the words of a personal God who is totally committed to His children. "I have called you by name," He says. "I know you. You are a special, unique child whom I have created. I know all about you. And I care about all the minute details of your life."

These are more than just the words of a perfect parent, for with them God gives us what no earthly parent can—the promise of His continual protective presence. God doesn't tell us that we won't pass through the waters of trial or walk through the fires of personal tragedy, but He does tell us that we won't be destroyed by them. Why? Because He will be right there beside us, surrounding us with His love and strengthening our spiritual stamina.

I have read these verses many, many times, and have claimed their promises not only for myself, but also for those I love—particularly for my children. Though I do as much as I can to protect my children from harm and unhappiness, I know that my protection is limited. Beyond that, I have to put my faith in God's promise that He will never allow them to go through any trial or danger alone. He will grip their little hands and help them through. He will make their spirits strong. In that, I rest.

The Helpful Hindrance

I can't end this chapter without mentioning another great spiritual truth. Not only will temptations and trials be unable to destroy those who trust in God, but those trials may actually bring about good in our lives.

"Consider it all joy, my brethren, when you encounter various trials, knowing that the testing of your faith produces endurance. And let endurance have its perfect result, that you may be perfect and complete, lacking in nothing" (James 1:2-4). If we want to be mature, strong, balanced, and able to stand up to the crises of life, what must we do? We must learn to handle our trials and temptations in such a way that they will contribute to our growth.

The Bible is filled with examples that illustrate this point. Paul speaks openly of his physical handicap. Though Scripture never reveals what it was, it was apparently something very grievous that contributed to the difficulty of his ministry.

Second Corinthians 12:8-10 records Paul's words concerning this "thorn":

Concerning this I entreated the Lord three times that it might depart from me. And He has said to me, "My grace is sufficient for you, for power is perfected in weakness." Most gladly, therefore, I will rather boast about my weaknesses, that the power of Christ may dwell in me. Therefore I am well content with weaknesses, with insults, with distresses, with persecutions, with difficulties, for Christ's sake; for when I am weak, then I am strong.

Paul recognized the profound truth that his weakness was the perfect showplace for God's divine power. He realized too that his weakness in the flesh forced him to become stronger in the Spirit. It kept him from boasting in his own strength and forced him to depend on God's strength. Therefore, he welcomed his "thorn" and all other hardships that weakened him, for he valued the strength of his spirit far more than the strength of his body.

Earlier I mentioned Jody, my friend who suffers from leukemia. Not long ago, I asked her to tell me about some of the important lessons she has learned through her illness. Her response illustrates Paul's point beautifully.

For years, my most troublesome sin was that of running ahead of the Lord. When I came up with an idea, instead of taking it to the Lord to see if it was a good one, I just moved ahead with it according to my own plans. I had plenty of energy and I like to get things done. I didn't have time to consult the Lord. Consequently, though I didn't realize it at the time, I did a lot of things that were not in accordance with the will of God. I manipulated people and rationalized behavior in an attempt to accomplish my supposedly "God-given goals." Unfortunately, they were anything but God-given, and they were done not in God's strength, but in my own.

My illness, however, has forced me to slow down and listen to the Lord. I no longer have the energy to head out in a multitude of directions. I can only concentrate on a few things, so I have to make sure they're the right ones. As long as I'm pursuing God's goals, I have the energy I need to accomplish them, but as soon as I venture off on my own, I'm in trouble. I can't rely on Jody's strength anymore, for Jody's strength is gone. I have no choice but to wait for God's direction and depend entirely on His energizing power.

Sometimes I think God allowed me to have leukemia just so I would learn to slow down and wait on Him. I don't think He could trust me with all my energy—I was making too many mistakes, chasing my own ideas—so He had to take it away. Maybe someday He'll be able to trust me with it again. Wouldn't that be great! But if not, that's fine with me. I know He'll give me just the strength I need to do what He wants me to do. And that's all I really want.

Jody has allowed her illness to bring about good in her life. She has learned, along with Paul, that God's power is perfected in human weakness and that His grace is always sufficient. Like Paul and Jody, we should live with the vivid knowledge that our lives are not our own, but rather gifts from the Sustainer. We ought to have the quiet assurance that though the effects of this sinful and imperfect world may touch our bodies and our lives, we are still, ultimately, in the hands of the Lord.

This I Know

This chapter has been very difficult for me to write because there is so much about God's sustaining power that I don't understand. It's hard to deal with this subject without drifting over into the problem of suffering and evil. If God is good and almighty, if He's benevolent and omnipotent, why does He permit pain and trouble? Why isn't His protection absolute? In fact, why do we need protection in the first place? Why is there evil?

I know that philosophers and theologians have grappled with these questions for thousands of years, and I have read many of their learned explanations. I have even added my own support for the value of suffering by pointing out how it can bring about good in our lives. But still, deep down inside, I am left with nagging questions. Like Habakkuk, sometimes I wonder what God is doing.

Why has His sustenance and protection been so evident in my life, while others seem to be caught in the vicious grasp of a twisted world? Why does He choose that some should live and some should die? Why are whole tribes and nations wiped out by famines and floods, by earthquakes and hurricanes? Why doesn't He intervene? Or does He, in ways unseen by men?

I don't know the answers to these questions. Maybe someday I will know them, if God chooses to reveal them to me. But in the meantime, there are many things that I *do* know. And for those things I can worship God.

I know that without the energizing touch of God's omnipotent hand, nothing that we see or feel or hear or sense would be in existence. God is the Creator. For that I can worship Him.

I know that without His source of power, the universe could not continue to exist. He is the Sustainer, the one who keeps it going, who "holds it all together." For that I can worship Him.

I know that God provides food and shelter for me, far beyond the extent of my needs. For that I can worship Him.

I know that He has restored my soul during times of drought, protected me from overpowering temptations, and strengthened me in times of trial. These are all signs of His constant and loving intervention in my life, and for them I can worship Him.

I know that He will never remove His presence from me, and never make me face heartache and grief alone. For that I can worship Him.

Job had a lot of questions about pain and suffering until He came face-to-face with the reality of God's wisdom and power displayed in the created order. The same is true for me. I know that God's wisdom is so far beyond the wisdom of human thought that we are silly to question Him. I know that He is infinitely more powerful than the evil which we see operative in this world today. And I know that He is sovereign, and someday we will see the full disclosure of His sovereignty. He will no longer have to sustain us against temptation or trial. Evil will be overthrown, and the need for protection will become obsolete.

What a day that will be for all who have submitted to the Lord—a day of freedom, of rejoicing, of celebration, of worship!

But we don't have to wait for that day to rejoice or to worship. We have *today* the promise of our Sustainer that He will keep us in His tender care until the day He calls us home.

9
God, the Giver of Eternal Life

When does eternal life begin? Most people probably think that eternal life begins at the moment of death, when we are ushered from earthly life into the afterlife, but is that true? What does the Bible say? "And the witness is this, that God has given us eternal life, and this life is in His Son. He who has the Son has the life; he who does not have the Son of God does not have the life" (1 John 5:11-12).

These verses don't indicate that eternal life is something that we enter into at the time of bodily death. Rather, it is something that we possess *now*. It is a life to which we are born the moment we become true Christians.

Most of us look at death as the turning point of our existence. We see it as the crisis point, where we either face eternal life or eternal damnation. But death is not really the turning point. At the time of our physical birth, we begin a journey destined for damnation. We are born into sin and in that birth we incur the wrath of God which dooms us to eternal punishment. If we die in that sin, without repenting and claiming Christ's forgiveness, we will merely be taking the final step down the path of damnation that we have trod since birth. Death is no turning point. It is just the last step along an already established path.

If, however, we repent of our sins and lay ourselves sincerely upon the mercies of God, then we are at a turning point. At the moment of our decision to accept God's plan of redemption, we turn from the path that leads to inevitable and final destruction onto the path of life. We no longer walk as dead men, but as men and women who have been awakened to eternal life.

At that point, we begin to walk in fellowship with God, and as we mature as Christians our fellowship with Him grows sweeter and closer. At death we take the final step along the path of fellowship with God. We are freed of the bodies that hinder us and the sin that plagues us, and we walk with full assurance and joy into the presence of God, a presence that we have already known in a limited sense, but will then know fully. Death is no turning point; it is merely the passageway into a fuller dimension of the life we have already begun to live on earth.

Eternal Life Today
Eternal life begins at the point of our salvation, and continues past death into the life hereafter. When we talk about eternal life, then, we have to talk about two separate elements—first, the quality of life that we enjoy in this world, and second, the form of life that we will enjoy in heaven.

When we talk about a high quality of life on earth, we are not saying that Christians have been insulated from evil, or that they will always enjoy good health and material prosperity. We are saying, however, that even in the midst of the unavoidable troubles that touch our lives, we can enjoy a quality of inner life far superior to that experienced by nonbelievers. Psalm 1 says that the believer "will be like a tree firmly planted by streams of water," while the unrighteous man is "like chaff which the wind drives away" (Ps. 1:3-4).

Jesus said, "I come that they might have life, and might have it abundantly" (John 10:10). Contrary to what unbelievers often say, Jesus did not come to make life boring or unsatisfying. He created us, redeemed us, sustains us, and now He wants to give us a quality of life that cannot be matched.

Let's look at three of the benefits that God has given to assure us of an abundant life: direction, purpose, and peace.

A Light for Our Path

Our church has a beautiful summer camp located in the dense forest lands of upper Michigan. Situated on the banks of the Tahquamenon River, it is definitely a "rustic" camp—no electricity, no running water, no indoor plumbing. Naturally, certain items are requirements for packing—mosquito repellent, rain gear, warm clothes, heavy sleeping bags, and of course, a flashlight. When the sun goes down and clouds cover the moon, campers get an entirely new understanding of the word *darkness.* With no streetlights, headlights, or lamps shining through cabin windows, there is an overwhelming darkness. You literally cannot see your hand in front of your face.

One year Bill and I both went to camp without flashlights. On clear nights when the moon was full, we were fine. We managed to make our way easily from place to place. But one night, the clouds completely hid the moonlight. As we anticipated our journey from the lodge to our cabin at the other end of the camp, we knew we were in for trouble.

At first, the darkness didn't stop us. We managed to stumble down the wooded path, brushing bushes and bumping into tree trunks, but when we got to the creek we really had problems. Where was the little bridge? We knew it had to be close. But *where?* We inched slowly to the left, then to the right, clinging to each other for balance, but inevitably tripping over each other's feet—and still we couldn't find that evasive little bridge.

Finally, we actually had to call for help. How humiliating! In the distance, we could hear the hearty laughter of those who had heard of our predicament. And even in the faint light of his flashlight, we could see the teasing smile on the face of our "heroic" rescuer.

But what if there had been no "rescuer"? What if there had been no light for our path? We would have wandered around all night, groping desperately in the darkness.

That is just the way it is for those who ignore the light of God's Word. They don't know who God is or where truth is. They walk around in the dark, hoping to find their way and maybe even thinking that they have, but they are misguided and lost.

Christians, however, need not be lost in darkness. The psalmist says, "Thy Word is a lamp to my feet, and a light to my path" (Ps. 119:105). In God's Word, we learn about morals and ethics and values. We learn how to handle crisis and disappointment. We learn how to relate to people and to God. We learn how to plan for the future. In short, we get the direction we need to live satisfying, God-pleasing lives.

Growing up in a family that loved to sail, I learned early the value of using a navigation chart. To sail through unknown water without a chart, where reefs may rest hidden beneath innocent-looking waters, is to take unnecessary risks and leave oneself open to unnecessary dangers. The sailor needs a chart. It is the only way to avoid disaster.

So also the Christian needs the Word of God. In a world that offers faulty answers to crucial questions, and relativity when we need absolutes, we *must turn* to the Word of truth—not so we can live lives of restricted pleasures and perpetual boredom, but so we can live lives of fullness and abundance.

A Reason to Live

"And the winds shall say: Here were a decent godless people, their only monument an asphalt road and a thousand lost golf balls." In these few, cryptic words, T.S. Eliot depicted the sense-lessness that characterizes a generation of people living without purpose. People who don't know where they came from or where they're going or what they should do in the meantime. People without direction and purpose who live lives of futility and quiet despair.

But such need not be true for the Christian. Throughout Scripture, we read universal calls to meaningful action. Any Christian who does not have a sense of purpose has not studied these revealed truths.

"He has told you, O man, what is good; and what does the Lord require of you but to do justice, to love kindness, and to walk humbly with your God!" (Micah 6:8) If we can think of no other worthy goal, surely we can find purpose in this verse.

What does it mean to *do justice*? It means that we walk in

integrity, according to the principles of Scripture, we treat others fairly, and defend those who have been taken advantage of.

And what does it mean to *love kindness?* It means that we should be sensitive, loving, and caring. We should be people who see needs and take action to meet them. We should be servants, using what we have been given for the benefit of others.

It's easy to develop a sense of futility when so much of our time is taken up with mundane chores. But how much more meaningful our work would be—whether we're preparing dinner or shopping or fulfilling our responsibilities to customers or employers—if we viewed each move, each word, and each encounter as an opportunity to show kindness to someone.

Finally, Micah 6:8 tells us to *walk humbly with our God.* To walk with someone means that where they go, we go. To walk humbly means that where they *lead,* we *follow.* One who has a "low" view of God will find it hard to walk humbly with Him. But one who has caught even a glimpse of His majesty and holiness will know that there is no higher goal than to walk with God in humble obedience.

Consider also this statement of purpose: "And you shall love the Lord your God with all your heart, and with all your soul, and with all your mind, and with all your strength. . . . You shall love your neighbor as yourself" (Mark 12:30-31). From these words of Jesus we find the greatest commandment, and for the Christian, the greatest purpose in life. We are to love God with all our emotions, with all our intellect, and with all our energy, and we are to share His love with our neighbors.

Paul reveals another godly purpose when he tells us to be "steadfast, immovable, always abounding in the work of the Lord, knowing that your toil is not in vain in the Lord" (1 Cor. 15:58). Our purpose is to build the kingdom of God. That doesn't mean that we have to be involved in "full-time Christian service." But we must remember to do all our work "as to the Lord" (Col. 3:23, KJV), and take advantage of each opportunity to minister to others for the sake of Christ. And what is the promise? That our work will not be done in vain.

It's easy to take for granted the privilege of having a meaningful purpose in life. Sometimes I even begin to slip into feelings of self-pity. I think, *There is so much to do. I'm so tired. There are so many needs to be met, so many choices to make.* I actually complain about the great sense of purpose that God has given me.

At other times, I forget my purpose entirely. I focus on the mundane tasks to be completed, or on the demanding responsibilities to be fulfilled, and I forget *why* I'm doing them. I look at the short-term difficulties and ignore the long-range goals.

What a foolish thing for a Christian to do. We are intimately related to the God of the universe, who has given us worthy, *eternal* goals. While the "asphalt road" will disintegrate in the inevitable destruction of time, our goals met in the purposes of the Spirit will stand forever.

God has put us all in different situations and given us different personalities and abilities, but He has given each of us the goals of godliness and service. If we are open and willing, He will show us how we can meet those goals right where we are, in ways designed just for us.

More Than the World Can Give

Throughout the book, I've mentioned several of my favorite peaceful experiences—walking through the woodlands, relaxing in the white sand on the shores of Lake Michigan, and sitting on the bow of a sailboat, mesmerized by the constant up and down swells of the waves. I have also experienced peace-filled moments riding up the side of a mountain in a ski lift, enjoying the beauty of the snow-covered mountains and feeling the warmth of the winter sun. I have even experienced peaceful moments in the privacy of my own living room, curled up in an easy chair with a good book.

. I have been fortunate to have enjoyed many such peace-filled moments, and I have treasured them greatly. But I have also learned that this kind of peace is very fragile and easily destroyed. The quiet walk through the woods can be disrupted by a sudden spring rain. The peaceful moments on the sandy beaches can be ruined by an army of flies that settles by my picnic basket.

The quiet sailboat ride can be interrupted by the chilling spray that crashes over the side as the wind and waves increase. The ride in the ski lift can lose its appeal when the temperature drops below the comfort zone. And the quiet moments in the easy chair will undoubtedly be destroyed when the children wake from their naps.

Yes, these peaceful moments, while found only with great difficulty, are so easily lost. Circumstances can change in an instant, and with the change often comes the destruction of peace. It is important, therefore, that we do not confuse these "peaceful moments" with the kind of peace that God offers us. He wants to give us a true inner peace that *lasts* because it is not a condition of external circumstances, but rather a condition of our hearts.

Jesus said, "Peace I leave with you; My peace I give to you; not as the world gives, do I give to you. Let not your heart be troubled, nor let it be fearful" (John 14:27). Paul writes, "And the peace of God, which surpasses all comprehension, shall guard your hearts and your minds in Christ Jesus" (Phil. 4:7).

The peace that God promises us surpasses human understanding. We cannot create it in a laboratory. We can't manufacture it synthetically. We can't even describe it adequately. But it can fill our hearts and minds regardless of our circumstances, difficulties, or problems.

To define *peace* in negative terms, we would say that it is the absence of war. From that definition, we can assume that if we are not experiencing peace, it is because we are warring—with God, with others, with ourselves, or with our circumstances.

The Bible helps us end our war with God by teaching us of repentance and submission. When we acknowledge Jesus Christ as our Saviour, we hoist the white flag of surrender. Then each time we confess our sins and ask for God's forgiveness, we lift the flag a little higher. Every true Christian knows the gnawing discomfort that accompanies disobedience. But when we confess our sins and submit to His will, we reestablish our fellowship with Him and restore our peace.

The Bible helps us end our war with others by giving us specific guidelines for our behavior in relationships. The Bible teaches us to communicate honestly and openly, but with sensitivity. It teaches us to be concerned with other people's needs. It teaches us to say "I was wrong" or "I'm sorry." It teaches us to be courteous, gracious, hospitable, kind, and gentle. If we follow these guidelines, we can establish relationships that are mutually pleasurable and characterized by peace.

The Bible helps us end our war with ourselves by establishing our value as children of God. With this knowledge, we can gain the confidence to use our God-given abilities, and we can develop the maturity to admit and accept our limitations.

The Bible tells us how to end our wars with God, with others, with ourselves, and finally, with our circumstances. We learn that the specific things that happen to us are not nearly as important as our reactions to them. Difficult situations can be effective character-building tools if we allow God to work through them.

When we have peace with God, we can enjoy the intimate communion that our souls desire. When we have peace with others, we can enjoy the earthly fellowship that makes life full. When we have peace with ourselves, we can be serene and quietly confident. When we have peace with our circumstances, we can find delight in little things and see the blessings of life.

We would be fools to live any life but the life of peace. Why be at war when we can have the peace "which surpasses all comprehension"?

Our Future Destination

Eternal life starts the minute we bow to Christ. But salvation does not erase all our problems. We will still suffer from time to time, and know pain and heartache and death. But through it all, we can live meaningful, joyful lives if we take advantage of the gifts offered by God—the gifts of direction, purpose, and peace.

But these are not the only gifts that God chooses to give us. He also offers the promise of a future residence in heaven, the place of eternal perfection. And in this promise we find the hope of a future life that so transcends our lives here that we can't even imagine it.

Unfortunately, many people think that belief in the afterlife is too naive, too unscientific for our sophisticated times. The trage-dy is that in throwing out their belief in the afterlife, they have also lost their sense of immortality. They have lost their connection with eternity.

Ecclesiastes 3:11 tells us that God has set eternity in our hearts, but modern man has denied that connection with eternity, and in denying that, his life has become meaningless. In the philosophy of existence that denies the survival of the soul, man becomes a short-lived speck of light, glimmering faintly for a moment, only to be forever extinguished by death, which returns man to the dust of this tiny planet.

We Christians cannot prove the survival of the soul or personal-ity of man anymore than the skeptics can prove otherwise. How-ever, in the overwhelming evidence for the resurrection of our Lord Jesus Christ, we find adequate reason to believe in our own eternal survival.

Few Christians really know what they believe about heaven. Most of us have just a smattering of information, some biblical, and some based on uneducated tradition that amounts to little more than wishful thinking. We casually express our belief in heaven, but our belief is so poorly supported and so seemingly insignificant that it hardly affects us.

How can we justify our limited interest in a subject that obvi-ously meant so much to our Lord? Part of the Good News that Christ brought to this world is that death no longer has any control over us. He has defeated death, and if we live in Him we too will overcome death. We can therefore be free from fear. We can have hope for the future. And we can view death not as our final enemy, but as the vehicle that will carry us into the land of promise.

The New Jerusalem

In any discussion of heaven, it is crucial to point out in the very beginning that *heaven,* whatever it is, must be fundamentally different from anything else that we know. It is a *spiritual* environ-ment, unhindered by the dimensions of time and space which limit our earthly lives. Therefore, when biblical writers describe heaven, they use allegories and metaphors. They describe spiritual realities in physical terms. Consequently, they gave us not a scientific account of heaven, but rather a creative description of what heaven is like.

It is important to keep this interpretational truth in mind because many people who have rejected the idea of heaven have done so because they erroneously looked at figurative language as if it were to be taken literally. For example, we read in the Book of Revelation that heaven is a city. But no credible biblical scholars really believe that out in space somewhere is a city limit sign that says *Heaven,* flanked by city guides who pass out maps and give population information.

Most scholars believe that the Apostle John used the concept of a city to convey the idea that heaven is a community of believers gathered together in a certain place. It is not a *place* as we would think of it, of course, because it is in a nonmaterial setting. We cannot describe it as up or down or located in some hidden corner of the universe, as yet undiscovered. But it is a place in the sense that it is where God is, and somehow He will bring together all who have become His children to dwell with Him there.

This concept is important because it negates the erroneous concept that heaven is merely a state of mind, or a peaceful vacuum of nothingness. These vague attempts to justify the concept of immortality without giving it concrete reality having nothing to do with the biblical heaven. Heaven is not a creation of man's imagination. It is a place beyond the comprehension of human thought, where believers of all ages will dwell together in fellowship and unity, beholding the unveiled glory of God.

Scripture indicates that believers will be given new, spiritual bodies, and that in heaven we will recognize those whom we have known in this life. David Winter says:

In heaven we will live, and live more fully and satisfyingly than ever before. And that life will involve all the really important elements of what we know as life: relationships, development, knowledge, communication . . . and all in the same mode as life on earth: personality expressed through a body. The differences are enormous, but do not diminish in any way the quality of life. We shall recognize our loved ones, but more by who they *are* than by what they look like. But better than that, we shall know them with a depth and insight and love unimaginable in our present human existence. Life will be transformed in the presence of its Creator and Sustainer (*Hereafter,* Harold Shaw Publishers and the Christian Book Promotion Trust, pp. 77-78).

Think of the fellowship you now enjoy with your closest friend or your spouse or your children. Now imagine that same joyous fellowship being elevated to a place where unity is never diminished by discord, where love is never threatened by jealousy, where communication is never hindered by misunderstanding, where thought and behavior are never in any way affected by sin. Imagine such fellowship!

Just as scholars accept the figurative meaning of *city* in reference to heaven, so they accept the figurative explanation for the *streets of gold.* Winter says, "Heaven is no more literally made of gold and precious stones than the Promised Land of Canaan literally flowed with milk and honey, but the image being presented is clear enough in both cases" (*Hereafter*, pp. 74-75). Heaven will be beautiful! In fact, it will be the place of ultimate beauty. There we will see God's handiwork displayed in all its glory, untainted by the ravages of sin and greed and exploitation.

The Bible tells us that this heavenly city will also have walls. What does this imply? That our heavenly residence will be a protected place. In ancient days, the strength of a city rested in the strength of its walls. They were its security, its shield against intrusion and attack. Our heavenly environment will likewise be protected, not by walls made with human hands, but by the power of God's presence. Not one speck of evil will be allowed within its walls (Rev. 22:15; 21:27).

Imagine an existence without fear. Without pain. Without grief. In this world, evil spills over into our lives. It touches the righteous as well as the unrighteous. But nowhere in heaven's walls will there be the slightest crack to let in evil. As the Apostle John said, "He shall wipe away every tear from their eyes; and there shall no longer be any death; there shall no longer be any mourning, or crying, or pain; the first things have passed away" (Rev. 21:2-4).

The Bible also tells us that in this city there are dwelling places which Jesus is preparing for those who will join Him (John 14:2). Imagine the significance this message had for the band of itinerant preachers to whom He spoke. They slept on the roadsides. They slept on mountainsides and in damp caves. They slept in the bottoms of boats. What joy they must have had in knowing that someday they would be wanderers no more.

In his vision, John also talks about the white robes worn by the saints of heaven (Rev. 6:11). Throughout Scripture, white is the symbol of purity; and in heaven, at least, we will be clothed with the white robes of Christ's righteousness. I admit that this is one of my favorite portions of John's description. How anxious I am to be pure and sinless—to please God continually!

The Bible also speaks about the harps of heaven (14:2). In the past, many musical experts considered the music of the harp to be the purest and most beautiful. Some musicians still think that's true. From a theological standpoint, however, the importance is not the specific musical form, but rather the implication that music will be an important part of heaven.

One of my favorite experiences is to stand in the midst of the congregation at our church and join with other believers as we sing words of worship. Imagine what it will be like to hear the voices of millions of saints as we sing in worship to our Passover Lamb: "Worthy is the Lamb that was slain to receive power and riches and wisdom and might and honor and glory and blessing" (5:12).

The Apostle Peter writes, "And when the Chief Shepherd appears, you will receive the unfading crown of glory" (1 Peter 5:4). A crown is the universal symbol of royalty and victory. At last, we will know triumph. The battle will be over, the victory won!

How can we possibly comprehend what it will be like to see the Father and the Son in all their glory? As we study and meditate on the existence and reality of God, we catch little glimpses that help us to cling to the reality of the unseen. But one day we will see Him as He is, and He will be more magnificent than anything we have ever imagined.

Our Spiritual Stockpile

"I don't want to be one of those people who gains the whole world and loses their own soul," said the wealthy woman executive to my husband. "I don't want to be that foolish. Tell me what to do."

In the lengthy conversation which ensued, my husband shared with this woman what it means to be a sinner before a holy God, what Christ accomplished on our behalf at Calvary, and how we can by faith enter into a relationship with the God of the universe and be assured that we have moved "from condemnation into life." At the end of the conversation, they prayed together and the woman acknowledged her sin and her need for Jesus.

In the four days that followed, this woman gave ample confirmation of her sincere commitment to Christ in conversations with family and friends. On the fifth day, she died in her sleep—a victim of the cancer that had ravaged her body for years.

On the evening of the following day, when Bill and I visited the funeral home, this woman's 15-year-old daughter asked us the million dollar question. *What is heaven like?* To a young girl who had just lost the mother she adored, the answer to that question was the only answer that could offer her any comfort. How glad we were to tell her that heaven is real, that it is prepared specifically for people like her mother who place their trust in Christ, and that it is a wonderful, glorious place in which to spend eternity.

Just days before, Shauna, our seven-year-old daughter, had ended her bedtime prayers with these words: "And God, please take care of Mark. Help him to remember the good part—that his mom is in heaven." To our little girl, whose classmate had just lost his mother, that was the only thing to hang onto—that death for the Christian does indeed have a "good part."

This morning I sat in a Bible study class in which the discussion centered on the difficulty that many people have in sharing their faith with others. As I listened to the discussion, I couldn't help but think that part of the reason we are so slow to share our faith is that we simply don't realize what we have in Christ. We haven't taken stock of our spiritual wealth.

We have taken for granted what it means to know that we are planned creations of a loving God. We have taken for granted the priceless gift of redemption. We have taken for granted the personal intervention of our all-powerful Sustainer. And we have forgotten that death is not the final victor. In Christ, we shall live forever!

10
Solitude —
A Personal Sanctuary

For some people, solitude is something to be feared. It implies open expanses of time—unscheduled moments and hours—that *must* be filled, lest they unnerve them with their silence and oppress them with their emptiness. But for the Christian, solitude is an opportunity to be sought and cherished. It is a time to enjoy the reality of God's presence.

It is not, however, solitude itself that leads us to precious moments of fellowship with the Lord. It is what we *do* in those brief moments snatched from our busy days that determines what will happen to them.

I have found during the last year that there are three elements, that if incorporated into my moments of solitude, will almost always assure me a valuable time of worship, growth, and communion with God. These are meditation, memorization, and music.

Biblical Meditation
For many people, the word *meditation* holds a negative connotation because of its frequent association with Eastern religions. When we think of meditation, we think of Buddhists who chant words and phrases to gain the attention of dead idols, or Hindus who enter meditative trances and pierce their bodies with skewers or walk on hot coals. Or we think of misguided Americans who

pay large sums of money to purchase their personal "mantras," or who engage in other kinds of mental calisthenics that combine Eastern religion and popular psychology.

The basic assumption of Eastern religion is that we are not personal beings, but merely parts of the great "impersonal universe." The goal of Eastern meditation, therefore, is the obliteration of the personality, so that the meditating individual can become "nothing" and be absorbed into the impersonal universe where he will supposedly find peace.

Because of the pervasiveness of this Eastern definition of meditation, many Christians have ignored meditation.

As they see it, meditation is a dangerous activity, a frightful "giving over" of the mind to unhealthy ideas. But can we so easily ignore the concept?

Let's see what the Bible says about meditation.

Let the words of my mouth and the *meditation* of my heart be acceptable in Thy sight, O Lord, my rock and my redeemer (Ps. 19:14).
When I remember Thee on my bed, I *meditate* on Thee in the night watches (63:6).
O how I love Thy law! It is my *meditation* all the day (119:97).
This book of the law shall not depart from your mouth, but you shall *meditate* on it day and night, so that you may be careful to do according to all that is written in it (Josh. 1:8).

These are but a few of the scriptural references to meditation. Obviously it is a concept that we can't ignore. But what is biblical meditation?

To *meditate* means "to contemplate; ponder; to dwell in thought; to muse; to reflect; to cogitate; to weigh in the mind; to appraise; to study." *Meditation* can be defined as "close or continued thought." Each of these definitions implies the careful directing of thought on a given subject. It implies the conscious, intelligent use of the mind. It is not a meaningless repetition of words as encouraged in Eastern thought or forbidden in Scripture ("do not use meaningless repetition," Matt. 6:7), but rather a deliberate focusing of the mind on a predetermined subject.

Biblical meditation is the conscious, intelligent focusing of the mind on spiritual truth. In his excellent tape "True Biblical Meditation" (Liberation Tapes, Lubbock, Texas), Ron Carlson says that meditation must be centered on three essential elements if it is to be constructive and God-honoring. First, it must be founded upon the nature and character of God. Second, it must incorporate the study of God's Word and the application of that Word to life. And third, it must focus on the centrality of Jesus Christ.

The Nature and Character of God

Psalm 145:5 says, "On the glorious splendor of Thy majesty, and on Thy wonderful works, I will meditate," and in the remainder of the chapter the psalmist does just that. He mentions specifically God's greatness, His mighty acts, His power, His goodness, His righteousness, His grace, His mercy, His loving-kindness, His glory, His sovereignty, His sustaining power, and His nearness to those who call upon Him. In short, the author focuses on God's attributes.

I have thought long and hard on the attributes of God. At first, they were just words—words that described a Being so far beyond my comprehension that they were almost meaningless. They didn't grab my attention. They didn't move me to worship.

So I began to pray in earnest that God would use His Word to give me a meaningful picture of Himself, a picture that would move me. I concentrated on His attributes. I studied them. I *meditated* on them. I asked myself questions about them. Why is this attribute important? What if God were not that way? How has God displayed this particular quality of His Being to me in a personal way?

"Exalt the Lord our God, and worship at His footstool; holy is He" (Ps. 99:5). As I meditated on God's holiness, I pictured in my mind a brilliant white light, emanating from a single source and radiating in an infinite circle. As I imagined myself standing in the penetrating light of His holiness, I realized that my sins stood out as ghastly stains, and I was moved to confess my sins and renew my commitment to obedience.

By incorporating imagination into my meditation, I was able to "see" myself in the light of God's perfection. Now, whenever I think of God's holiness, I am immediately reminded of who I am—a sinner who desperately needs the cleansing that only Christ can give.

Let me illustrate the value of meditation again by looking at the attribute of God's omnipotence. Isaiah 40:26 tells us that God created the stars, called them by name, and "because of the greatness of His might and the strength of His *power* not one of them is missing." What is one way that God has displayed His power? By filling the sky with stars. As I meditate on God's creative power, I try to envision the magnitude of space, with its unfathomable number of galaxies, each filled with billions of stars that were put in place by God.

As I focus on this mental picture, I am filled with wonder that the God whose power hung the stars in space could reach down in infinite love, and care for me. Why does He, the supreme Power behind all that is, love me, a tiny speck in a corner of His creation? I don't know why, but He does. And my meditation on the God of all power has brought me back to a wonderful appreciation of the God of all love. As I go through the rest of my day, I will be repeatedly uplifted by that thought. The mighty God of all power loves *me*!

A casual reading of a few empty words will never open our minds to the glory of our God. But a willing investment of thought and prayer and meditation may indeed do just that. It grieves me that it has taken me so long to catch a glimpse of God's glory. But at least in meditating on His attributes I have an effective means of educating my mind—and opening my eyes—to the wonders of my God.

The Word of God

Biblical knowledge that never works its way into our hearts and minds is useless. That's why so many Christians have the information that could lead to godliness, but don't live the lives that would attest to godliness.

One way to help scriptural truth find its way into our hearts and minds is to meditate on it. Meditating on Scripture involves the process of "rumination." To *ruminate* means "to bring to mind and consider again and again." Personally, I am quite happy with this definition, but *Webster's Dictionary* gives us further information. It tells us that ruminate means "to chew the cud; to chew again what has been chewed slightly and swallowed."

As much as I would like to ignore this part of the definition, I have to admit that the lowly cow has done much to aid my own understanding of rumination. She knows that food which is only slightly chewed will not be properly digested. Only that which she "brings back" and chews again will actually be assimilated into her system.

So it is with Scripture. When we read a verse for the first time, it may impress us with its truth and wisdom, but it will probably have little lasting effect on us. It will not be "assimilated into our system." But when we look at that verse again and again and consider what it means and how it applies to us, we will indeed be changed by it.

Join me in a brief meditation on Psalm 100:1-2:

Shout joyfully to the Lord, all the earth. Serve the Lord with gladness; come before Him with joyful singing.

A quick reading of these verses tells us that Psalm 100 is a psalm of worship, in which all people are exhorted to praise the Lord. But if you are like me, in the brief reading you probably learned little more than that.

As I read those two verses over and over again, however, I am impressed with the psalmist's emphasis on joy and gladness. Apparently, he is trying to tell us that worship ought to be offered to God in joy.

As I think about this, I ask myself, *Am I worshiping joyfully? If not, why? What have I allowed to rob me of the joy that I ought to find in worship? Am I forgetting about all that God has done for me? Am I forgetting about His love and mercy and grace? Am I so caught up in self-centeredness and self-pity that I have lost sight of my blessings?*

Convicted by my answers to these questions, I begin to silently enumerate my blessings and remind myself of the richness I enjoy as a Christian. As I do that, I am inevitably brought to joyful, heartfelt worship.

Throughout the Psalms and elsewhere in Scripture, we can find many passages that call us to exalt God; as we meditate on them, we will undoubtedly be directed into worship. But meditation can also lead us into obedience in other areas of life as well. For example, there was a time in my life when my words to my husband were frequently harsh and critical, so I decided to meditate on Ephesians 4:29: "Let no unwholesome word proceed from your mouth, but only such a word as is good for edification according to the need of the moment, that it may give grace to those who hear." There was absolutely no way that I could focus my attention on that verse repeatedly throughout the day without being changed by it. My speech *had* to be affected.

The epistles are particularly rich with verses perfect for meditation. As you read and study, pick out passages that apply to specific problems or needs in your life, and begin to meditate on them. As you fill your mind with their truth, your behavior will begin to comply with the directives given in God's Word.

Jesus Christ

True biblical meditation focuses on the character and nature of God, on God's Word, and finally on Jesus Christ. Paul's desire for the Christians at Colosse was "that their hearts may be encouraged, having been knit together in love, and attaining to all the wealth that comes from the full assurance of understanding, resulting in a true knowledge of God's mystery, that is, *Christ Himself, in whom are hidden all the treasures of wisdom and knowledge*" (Col. 2:2-3).

Nothing will lead our hearts to worship more readily than meditating on *who* Jesus is and *what* He has done for us. In the reference section of my Bible, there is a list of the names given to Jesus in Scripture. Just a quick reading through this list provides a wealth of worship material. Consider a few of His names: Advocate, Almighty, Bread of Life, Bridegroom, Chief Cornerstone, Counselor, Deliverer, Door, Good Teacher, Great Shepherd, Holy One of God, King Eternal, King of Glory, Lamb of God, Life, Light, Messiah, Prince of Peace, Redeemer, Rock, Saviour, Truth, Way, Wonderful, Word of Life.

Christ Jesus is *all* of these and so much more. Think for a moment what it means to know that Jesus is our Great Shepherd. He guides us on the path of righteousness. He protects us from evil. He leads us to spiritual refreshment and provides for us the refuge of His presence. He has even laid down His life on our behalf. How blessed we are to be His sheep!

Or think of what it means to know that Jesus is Truth, that we have no need to seek elsewhere for absolutes or for wisdom. In Him we have "all the treasures of wisdom and knowledge" (Col. 2:3).

Or think about Jesus, the Deliverer. Meditate on all that He has delivered you from—fear, loneliness, condemnation, confusion, frustration—and all that He has given you in exchange—peace, freedom, eternal life, fellowship with God, joy, love, meaningful service.

Surely in the work and ministry of Jesus we can find much cause for worship.

The Night Watches

While meditation begins in solitude, it can be continued throughout the day, and can even be practiced by our subconscious minds as we sleep. According to Jim Downing, the instruction to meditate on the Word "day and night" was no idle command (Josh. 1:8). God, in speaking through Joshua thousands of years ago, knew what scientists have only learned recently. During sleep, the subconscious mind is active, *ruminating* the last thoughts that were placed in the conscious mind. Therefore, says Downing, we ought to allow our last waking thoughts to be centered on Scripture (*Meditation*, pp. 31-38).

This past summer I put Downing's suggestion to the test. I have always been more than a little fearful at night. Strange noises in the house can keep me awake for hours, and scary movies (which I no longer allow myself to watch) can ruin my sleep for days. As I mentioned in an earlier chapter, the kids and I spent ten weeks of the past summer in a lovely cottage on Lake Michigan. Bill visited us occasionally, but for the most part it was just the three of us—with no telephone and no streetlights. When we turned the lights out it was very dark, and the only sounds to be heard were the waves lapping against the beach and the wind rustling in the trees.

As might be expected, my first few nights there were horrible. I absolutely could not sleep. On the fourth night, I took Downing's advice and concentrated on one verse of Scripture as I tried to fall asleep. For obvious reasons, I chose Psalm 4:8: "In peace I will both lie down and sleep, for Thou alone, O Lord, dost make me to dwell in safety."

I don't know how many times I repeated that verse to myself during those weeks, but I do know that I enjoyed some very peace-filled evenings and many sleep-filled nights. Sometimes, I still woke up during the night. But I was surprised at the calmness I felt and the ease with which I drifted back to sleep.

Memorization

When I first became serious about worshiping the Lord, I felt very inadequate. I didn't know what to say or write. So I decided to learn from the words of the psalmists.

I began by memorizing Psalm 100. Only five verses long, it is short enough to be memorized easily and recited in its entirety in less than a minute. How has this helped me in worship? By giving me a ready arsenal of words that can flash through my mind at any time and turn my thoughts toward God. For example, I might be driving the car or washing the dishes when these words will come to mind. "Know that the Lord Himself is God; it is He who has made us, and not we ourselves. We are His people and the sheep of His pasture" (v. 3). As I recite those words, I focus my attention on God, the Creator and the Good Shepherd, and with my words and my attitude I exalt Him.

Or perhaps verse 5 comes to mind: "For the Lord is good; His loving-kindness is everlasting, and His faithfulness to all generations." As I think about those words, I focus on God's loving-kindness and worship Him for it.

Two years ago I memorized the Book of Philippians. I worked on it a little each day and eventually was able to recite the entire book. It was that effort that impressed upon me the importance of memorization. Though I have seriously studied other sections of Scripture, no other portion has ever challenged and inspired me like the Book of Philippians.

Somehow that long process of reading and repeating those verses to myself over and over again caused them to seep into my mind and heart like no other words ever have. Though I can no longer recite the book as I once could, I am still drawn back to those verses regularly.

When I am tempted to be selfish, I think of Philippians 2:3-4: "Do nothing from selfishness or empty conceit, but with humility of mind let each of you regard one another as more important than himself; do not merely look out for your own personal interests, but also for the interests of others."

When I feel like complaining, I remind myself to "do all things without grumbling or disputing," and "to be content in whatever circumstances I am" (2:14; 4:11).

When I get discouraged or don't feel like persevering, I challenge myself to "press on toward the goal for the prize of the upward call of God in Christ Jesus" (3:14).

When I'm letting my joy slip, I say, "Rejoice in the Lord always; again I will say, rejoice!" (4:4)

When I'm tempted to worry, I think about these words: "Be anxious for nothing, but in everything by prayer and supplication with thanksgiving let your requests be made known to God" (4:6).

The connection between meditation and memorization is obvious. The Holy Spirit can be counted on to bring verses to our remembrance just when we need them, but He can only do so if we have committed them to memory.

Music

O come, let us sing for joy to the Lord. . . . Sing to the Lord a new song; sing to the Lord, all the earth. . . . Shout joyfully to the Lord, all the earth; break forth and sing for joy and sing praises. Sing praises to the Lord with the lyre; with the lyre and the sound of melody. With trumpets and the sound of the horn. Shout joyfully before the King, the Lord. . . . Come before Him with joyful singing. . . . I will sing of loving-kindness and justice, to Thee, O Lord, I will sing praises (Pss. 95:1; 96:1; 98:4-6; 100:2; 101:1).

Certainly we don't have to wonder how God feels about music. It is a valuable language of worship which ought to be used lavishly and joyfully. Throughout the history of the church this truth has been recognized, and to greater and lesser degrees, obeyed. With few exceptions, music has been an integral part of the corporate worship of most local congregations.

Music need not, however, be relegated only to corporate worship. We can also use music as a meaningful worship tool in our own private times with God. Let me illustrate.

It was a cool, crisp morning. I had just tidied the house and deposited Todd at pre-kindergarten. I knew I had to write while he was at school, since it would be my only quiet time that day, but I was tired and grumpy.

I had had a short night's sleep and the inconveniences of suitcase living were getting to me. The cold weather had snuck up on me, and I hadn't yet located the cold-weather suitcase, so we had a horrible time finding appropriate clothes for the kids to wear. By the time they were out the door and settled for the day, I was ready for a little rest and self-pity.

Dutifully, I sat down at the typewriter to write about "God, the Giver of Eternal Life," but no words came. My mind and my spirit were both dry. So I grabbed the closest cassette tape, slid it into the tape player, and made myself comfortable on the floor, waiting for the music to lull me into a much-needed sleep.

But I had picked up a Sandy Patti tape and the first song that played was a stirring arrangement of "We Shall Behold Him." Though I certainly had not planned to have a moving spiritual experience that morning, I was drawn into worship by the music. As Sandy sang of the white-robed Lamb, I imagined Him—in all His glory—and my spirit was renewed.

When the song was over, I rewound the tape and played it

again, letting every word sink in. When it ended, I was ready to wrote about our priceless hope of heaven.

Because music demands the involvement of both our intellect and our emotions, it is an excellent way to draw our whole being into communion with the Lord. And because music is such an effective communicating tool, it can sometimes reach us when other words can't. When we don't have the mental energy to concentrate on meditaton or memorization, we can be led into worship by music that focuses our attention on God.

Throughout my school years, I studied the flute and diligently practiced, first under my mother's watchful eye and later in obedience to my own inner motivation to excel and enjoy. During those years, I played my flute in church and even joined a musical group that presented sacred concerts. After I was married, I continued to play sporadically. No longer could I maintain my daily practice schedule, but I played as often as I could and used my talent as needed at our church. After my second child was born, however, my life held no more room for the luxury of making music. With a great deal of regret, I packed away my flute in the farthest corner of my closet.

Not long ago, however, while I was enjoying a time of personal worship, I decided to get out my flute. On a bookshelf I found an old psalter hymnal, and in the quiet of my bedroom I played the old hymns of praise, reading the words as I played the notes. I can't begin to tell you how much I enjoyed that. It was a far more satisfying use of my talent than I had ever experienced, because I really felt that my music was for God alone. I wasn't trying to impress anyone. I wasn't nervous about my performance. I was simply using the gift God had given me to exalt Him.

Probably many of you are frustrated musicians whose musical aspirations have been pushed aside by life's time-consuming details. Like me, you have relegated your musical talents to days gone by, when your regular practice schedule made your music a little purer and your confidence a little greater. But why not use those skills again and enjoy them? You may be able to put your talent to a more noble use than you ever did before.

Others may be beginners who feel that your music is not much of a gift to offer. But remember, worship is more a matter of heart than of art. When my four-year-old son sings "I love Jesus, I love Jesus, I love Jesus," to the tune of his choice, I think he brings tremendous pleasure to the heart of God.

Get Specific
When Bill first taught about worship, he suggested that we keep journals, and many people in our church have done so. A worship journal may contain records of answered prayer or insights gained in personal Bible study, but it is primarily a notebook in which we write down our thoughts about God and about worship. Most people include personal prayers of confession and prayers of exaltation similar to those written by the psalmists. Others include lists of all the "mighty works" that God has done in their lives. A worship journal may also include verses written out from memory, with an explanation of why that verse leads the writer to worship.

For me, one value of keeping a journal is that it aids in my concentration. When I sit in a chair and "just think" about something, my mind tends to wander. But when I'm writing down my thoughts, I'm forced to concentrate. If my mind begins to wander, I know it immediately and I can call it back to attention.

Another value is that the things I write when I am particularly aware of God's presence encourage me on the days that I feel spiritually dry and empty. On such days, I can look back through my journal, read the record of my own personal worship, and be reminded that God *is* real and *I do* have many reasons to worship Him.

Some people will be anxious to start a worship journal and will write freely. Others will find this form of communication very difficult and will be restrained in their writing, able to add only two or three lines each day. But either way, a worship journal provides a valuable record of our worship experiences.

Another thing to consider in regard to worship is location. It may be helpful to have a special worship location in your home. During the last six months, I have had to be very flexible in finding my worship location, but before we began this nomadic "journey," I did have a special location. It was by an upstairs window where I could see the morning sun.

If I couldn't enjoy my quiet moments in the morning, I moved to the other side of the house where I could enjoy the hot light of the afternoon sun, or the warm glow of the setting sun. There is a subjective and symbolic significance in the sunlight that aids me in focusing my attention on the Lord, and a fascinating beauty in the sky that reminds me of His glory and majesty.

While I gravitate toward windows, one of my closest friends prefers to spend her quiet worship moments in the darkest, most sheltered place in her house. She says it helps her close out the distractions of the world and reminds her of the need to come before God in humility and submission.

Obviously, there is no "right" place to worship God. As a matter of fact, to the true believer *every* place should be the right place. But if you find a special place—a personal sanctuary—that helps you develop the discipline of worship, go there often. If you learn to worship God more devoutly there, you will become a more enthusiastic worshiper elsewhere as well.

For Women on the Go

I cannot end this chapter without saying a few words to moms of little kids. At ages seven and four, my children are finally willing to give me a little time to myself. But I remember well the infant-toddler years when solitude was eagerly sought but seldom found.

If you fit in that category, I know what you're thinking. *Sure, this all sounds great. Meditation, memorization, and music. But I have no "quiet moments" to fill. I'm lucky to find time to speed-read John 3:16! The whole idea sounds good, but it's just one more expectation that leaves me frustrated and discouraged.*

Believe me, I know that frustration. No occupation is as demanding as the full-time responsibility of caring for kids. For busy mothers, solitude is an almost impossible task—but it's not *quite* impossible. There are ways to develop a meaningful devotional life and make great progress in the art of worship, even in the extra busy years.

First, consciously acknowledge worship as your ultimate priority in life. Yes, we are called to love our husbands and children and to meet their legitimate needs as best we can. But first we are called to be worshipers; we will never be the kind of wives and mothers we should be unless we learn to worship.

Second, refuse to make comparisons. Don't compare yourself with the woman who spends three hours a day in Bible study and writes a short novel in her worship journal. Adjust your expectations to meet the realities of *your* lifestyle. Don't give up your goal, and don't ever think you can use a busy schedule to justify nonworship, but *be realistic.* Be willing to take little steps, knowing that these little steps will lead to bigger steps later.

Third, be creative. The ideal picture of solitude is something like this: The dishes are washed and put away, the floor is swept and mopped, the kids are napping peacefully, and the smell of freshly baked apple pie drifts slowly from room to room. The meticulously coiffed, quiet-spirited mom sits comfortably in an easy chair, sipping her favorite herbal tea and gazing at God's creation clearly visible through her recently washed windows.

How idyllic. How serene. And how sickeningly unrealistic!

Seldom does real life contain such perfect scenes. But that's OK. Believe it or not, there are some very acceptable alternatives to perfection.

To begin, have a friend or baby-sitter care for you children for three hours on a given afternoon. During that time, go to a Christian bookstore and buy at least one good worship tape or album. (If you don't live near a Christian bookstore, send for mail order catalogues from Christian publishing houses.)

Then go to a library with your Bible and some index cards. Spend about 45 minutes reading through some psalms, underlining verses that encourage you to *worship*—verses that impress you with the greatness of God or remind you of what He has done for you. Then choose 8 to 10 of your favorites and write them on individual index cards.

Next, turn to another section of Scripture (preferably New Testament) and read it several times, underlining verses that *challenge* you. Again, write your favorite verses on index cards.

When you have completed this project you will have, on simple index cards, material to use for meditation and memorization for weeks to come. The next time you have a few moments of solitude to invest in worship, you won't have to waste time wondering where to begin. Just pick up the first card in your "worship packet" and the first card in your "challenging packet."

When you have thoroughly used up your verses, by meditating on and perhaps even memorizing them, make another trip to the library and replenish your supply of material.

When you begin your time of personal worship, start with confession. In silence, ask God to bring to mind anything you need to confess. Then jot down in your journal whatever He reminds you of.

Next, move on to two of your preselected verses. Read your worship verse, think about it, and write a brief response in your journal. Then do the same thing with your challenge verse.

If you use the same verses for several days, you might want to skip the journal writing on some occasions and work on memorization instead. Either way, you will be internalizing what you are reading. You can end your quiet moments with a time of prayer for yourself, your family, your church, etc. As you return to your busy routine, you can do so refreshed and uplifted. You might even want to listen to a worship tape as you ease your way from solitude back into "real" life.

Before we leave this subject, here are a few more suggestions that may help you make time for worship:

1. Tape your index cards in convenient places—beside the ironing board, above the kitchen sink, or on a table by your favorite rocking chair. A quick glance at the verse will center your mind on the Lord.

2. Make use of children's tapes and albums. The *Kids Praise* tapes by Maranatha are excellent. They can keep your kids happily entertained and also feed your own spirit as well.

3. Make arrangements with a trusted friend to exchange kids regularly—you take hers for three hours on Monday and she'll take yours for three hours on Wednesday. Use this extended free time to do additional Scripture study that you don't normally

have time to do. Or sit down at the piano and offer God the gift of your music. Or take a walk and enjoy the beauty of God's creation. We arrange child care for everything from hair appointments to shopping trips. Why not do so for worship?

4. Don't try to go through your whole worship routine at one sitting. If you have 10 minutes in the morning, use it as a time of confession. If you have 5 minutes after lunch, focus on your verses. Think about them during the rest of the day as you work, and perhaps later you will think of something about them to write in your journal.

5. The key to developing the discipline of worship in solitude is *planning*. Have your verses ready and easily accessible so that when your quiet moments come, you don't waste 10 minutes figuring out where to start. Keep your journal handy. Also keep your albums and tapes in a safe place, readily available.

Be organized. Be prepared. Be disciplined. Your efforts *will be rewarded.*

11
The Transforming Power

There's nothing more refreshing than an unhurried walk along the beach during a gentle rain. As you feel the cool raindrops sprinkle tenderly on your hot skin, you breathe in the freshly washed air and feel cleansed and renewed.

On the other hand, there's nothing more frustrating than driving through a torrential downpour. As you strain to see the unfamiliar landmarks through the blur of water on your windshield, and you feel the pressure of the tailgater behind you who apparently doesn't appreciate your turtle pace, you sigh in audible frustration and wonder, *When will this awful rain stop?*

That was my question as I carefully (and tearfully) made my way to my first writer's conference. The rain certainly didn't help my sagging spirits, but even a sunny sky would have been no match for my inner turmoil. I was a wreck! I hate facing new experiences anyway, but it was even worse since I had already missed half the conference. I felt like I was entering territory that was known and familiar to everybody but me. I alone was the outsider.

I had had every intention of attending the entire conference, but the combined pressures of overscheduling, packing (the first of our recent moves was fast approaching), baby-sitter problems and an unexpected illness kept me from attending the opening sessions. By the second day, however, I thought I was ready to hit the conference trail again, and I really felt that I needed the help and inspiration that the well-known speakers would offer. So, with pen and paper and an eagerness to learn, I headed out.

But I hadn't counted on the rain and getting lost and feeling so out of place. By the time I got to the conference center, I wanted to turn around and go home!

Just sit here for a moment, I told myself as I eased my car into the nearest packing place. *It's too late to turn back now. Pull yourself together.*

And that's exactly what I did. In the next few moments in the quietness of my car, I experienced a welcome transformation. My frazzled emotions were calmed and my spirit was lifted. I left the car refreshed, and walked into the morning sessions with a sense of quiet anticipation.

What did I do in those few quiet moments? Catch a quick catnap? Have a good cry? Read a pep talk on positive mental attitude? Breathe deeply and meditate on quiet pastures and rippling brooks? What "trick" did I use?

My "trick" was worship. I knew that I was caught in a downward spiral of negative thoughts, and that my only hope was to focus my attention on something more positive. So I consciously turned my thoughts to a song we sing frequently at church.

Lord, You're worthy to be praised, and I praise You.
Lord, You're worthy to bow down to, and I bow down to You.
Lord, You're worthy to be worshiped, and I worship You.
I praise You. I bow down to You. I worship You.*

As I thought about the words to that song, I was forced to pull my thoughts away from my own petty problems and focus on the One worthy to be worshiped. And as I worshiped Him, I was naturally drawn into confession. I had to confess my inordinate concern with temporal things. I had to confess my crabbiness

---

*Celeste Yohai, "The Worship Song," © 1980 by Maranatha! Music. All rights reserved. International copyright secured. Used by permission only.

toward my kids and my impatience with my husband. And I had to confess my self-pity, my selfishness, and my ungrateful attitude toward a God who had given me so much.

After I confessed these things, I experienced the joy of forgiveness. In that joy I thanked God for the gift of life, for my husband, for my children, for my home, my friends, my church, for the privilege of knowing and serving Him, and for the opportunity to attend the conference and be challenged and stimulated. I had a long list of things for which I could be thankful, and I got out of my car with a heart of gratitude and an eagerness to face the day.

John Burkhart says, "Worship is to be judged by whether and how it transforms those who worship" (*Worship,* Westminster Press, p. 32). If I go through all the proper forms of worship—if I follow the right steps and say the right words—and remain unchanged, I have not worshiped. I have merely walked through an empty ritual.

True worship transforms the worshiper. That is not, of course, its primary function. Its primary function is to honor God. But the result of true worship—the inevitable result—is the transformation of the worshiper.

I first approached worship aware that in worship I would honor God, but unaware of the transformation that would take place in my own life. I began to worship God as an act of obedience, as a necessary discipline of the Christian life. And there was tremendous pleasure in doing that. It is very satisfying to know that we are giving God that which He most desires—our worship and praise. But as I pursued the discipline of worship, I learned that we have much more to gain from it than just the satisfaction of pleasing God. As is so often the case, when we offer a gift to God (in this case, our worship), He gives us far more in return than we could ever have hoped for.

A New Perspective

One obvious result of true worship is that the worshiper gains a new perspective on life. When I consciously center my mind on the Lord and worship Him, the minor irritations of my life appear petty in comparison to the vast blessings I have received from the Lord. Instead of complaining and fretting about my problems, I thank God for His blessings.

I must confess that I am not naturally a positive person. I find it easy to look on the dark side of life. I'm always prepared with a complaint to meet every situation. I'm easily irritated. I tend more toward self-centered introspection than other-centered service. And I find it much easier to assume that I will fail at a given endeavor than I will succeed.

Does any of that sound familiar to you? Can you relate to my shameful confession? If so, be of good cheer! For I have found in worship the perfect antidote for this malady of mind and spirit that causes us to focus on the negative. In worship I have gained a new perspective on life, and in acquiring this new perspective I have found the freedom to cast off the chains of negative thoughts.

Throughout my adult years I have been haunted by three nagging problems. First, I have been unwilling to accept what I consider to be the "flaws" of my physical appearance. Second, I have been hindered by my lack of confidence and my sense of emotional weakness. And third, I have been pulled back and forth by the conflicting voices of human expectations.

Certainly, I am not alone in struggling with these issues. I know that many people are haunted by these negative perspectives. At best, they live with a nagging sense of dissatisfaction. At worst, they live in a perpetual state of unhappiness, disliking themselves and the lives they lead. They are crippled by low self-esteem, defeated by fear, and tyrannized by unrealistic expectations.

What Kind of Beauty?
In a society that places an incredible amount of emphasis on physical attractiveness, it's not hard to get caught up in the competitive game of comparisons. The unfortunate thing is that everyone who plays this game ends up a loser. We can always find someone who is prettier, slimmer, or more shapely than we are. There is always someone whose eyes are bigger and bluer, whose hair is bouncier, and whose smile is more intriguing. To

put it simply, there is *always* someone who looks better than we do.

I have played that game many times, and often I have wanted to shake my fist at God and say, *I hate the way You made me. Why did You do this?*

It's embarrassing to admit this, because I know these are not the words of a mature and sensible woman who knows her worth and has dedicated herself to the service and encouragement of others. But these words all too often describe my feelings. In this particular area, I am very immature and insecure, and I struggle daily with the problem of self-acceptance.

I have found, however, that during worship, when my mind is filled with the realization of God's infinite wisdom and love, it is impossible for me to shake my fist in anger against Him. It is impossible to question His judgment—not because I fear to do so, but because I realize that it is ludicrous to do so. It is crazy to shake my puny fist in the face of infinite wisdom. Who am I to say that I know a better way? That I could have created a better me?

It's almost laughable when you think about it. I, the creature, telling the Creator that He missed the mark when He made me. Only He knows His reasons for creating me just the way I am, and I have no cause to question Him. My only legitimate response is willing acceptance of His design, and in worship I make that conscious acceptance.

The amazing thing about this conscious decision to accept God's plan is that it does not carry with it a sense of defeat. It does contain an element of "giving up," but it is the giving up of a tiresome burden rather than the giving up of a prized belonging. By accepting God's plan, I realize that what the world tells me is ultimately "important" is not that important after all. It is "the hidden person of the heart, with the imperishable quality of a quiet and gentle spirit, which is precious in the sight of God" (1 Peter 3:4). God's desire for me is to live a life of service, and I need not be externally beautiful to serve. Focusing undue attention on my own imperfections is nothing more than a thinly veiled self-centeredness.

God is not anti-material. In other words, He doesn't deny the importance of our physical bodies. I believe that in order to please God, we must keep our physical bodies in good shape through proper eating, resting, and exercising. One of my personal goals is to become more disciplined in exercise so that I will look better and feel better. Though I do not have a weight problem, I do want to have a better toned body, and I want to have more energy and endurance. I also want to enjoy the mental "cleansing" that accompanies physical exertion.

But these healthy goals should never be used to justify an obsession with physical beauty. If we want to be godly, we must learn to be obsessed, not with those things that are merely temporal, but with those things that are eternal.

I thank God that He is "growing me up" in this regard. I thank Him for patiently teaching me truth and pointing out my errors. I have seen, in the last year, a definite shift in my attitude. I am less likely to find myself questioning God's wisdom in arranging my external characteristics, and more likely to find myself imploring His help in the development of my internal character. I spend less time comparing myself with fashion models and more time comparing myself with the model described in Galatians 5:22-23, that "beauty" who displays such outstanding qualities as love, joy, peace, patience, kindness, goodness, faithfulness, gentleness, and self-control.

I will never achieve the standard of physical beauty that would satisfy my natural, human desire. But I know that really doesn't matter. God is more concerned about the beauty of my inner life. As I worship Him and allow Him to change my perspective, I am finding that an unhealthy negativism is gradually giving way to a healthy acceptance of God's wisdom in creating me just as I am, and a greater desire to please Him by learning to love and serve and encourage others.

What about My Weakness?

My second nagging problem is my lack of confidence, and my timidity in using my abilities. In an earlier chapter, I mentioned my friend Jody's problem of moving ahead of God, aggressively pursuing her own ideas in her own strength. My problem is just the opposite. God could send me a leaflet from heaven telling me exactly what He wants me to do, and I would say, "Oh no, Lord. I couldn't do *that*. I'm weak. I would probably fall. Maybe another time."

I have spent an incredible amount of time telling God—and everyone else—what I can't do. In spite of the abundance of "cheerleaders" with which I have been blessed—family and friends to support, encourage, and "cheer me on"—I have managed to cling to my position of timidity and fear. I have managed to hide behind my cloak of defeatism.

For years, Bill and others have affirmed my ability to write, but always against the backdrop of my vehement denials. Though Bill was convinced that he saw in me the skills and personality tendencies that would lend themselves well to writing, I was equally convinced that he was wrong. Occasionally my conviction wavered and I began to believe him, but it never took long for me to come up with a thousand ways to negate his insight. He was wrong. I couldn't do it. I would fail.

So why am I writing this book? What happened to my extensive collection of well-used excuses? They were consumed in the fire of true worship. They turned to ashes in the presence of the Almighty God. When I came face-to-face with the God of all power, I realized that I could no longer plead the case of weakness. "Oh, so you're weak," God said. "That's great. Then I can tell you the same thing I told My friend Paul. My strength is made perfect in your weakness. My grace is sufficient for you. You see, I specialize in giving power to weak people!"

When we come before God in worship, we are forced to give up our insecurities and our timidity, and take from Him the gift of power. It's not the surface power that the world extols, a manipulative play of force that gives us a false superiority over others, but a power that flows from our confidence in the God who empowers us.

God's power allows us to step out and do what He asks us to do with quiet resolve. His power allows us to control our passions and our desires, so that we can live in obedience to God's Word.

His power allows us to stand up under pressure and cling to our principles even when we come under attack. The worshiping person is in contact with the God of all power, and through that contact flows the power that we need to live God-honoring lives.

Dan DeHaan said, "Find me a worshiper of God, and I will show you a stable man with his mind in control, ready to meet the present hour with refreshment from above" (*The God You Can Know,* Moody Press, p. 17). That is a perfect description of the life of power. How often do you feel "ready to meet the present hour"? We won't be ready unless our minds have been enriched by focusing on God in worship. Isaiah's famous response to God's call, "Here am I. Send me!" (Isa. 6:8) came after his vision of heavenly worship. Would he have been ready to respond with confidence to God's call had he not just joined with the heavenly creatures in exalting the Lord and submitting himself in humility before "the King, the Lord of hosts"? (v. 5) Probably not.

Hundreds of times during the writing of this book I have become panic-stricken. I have been alternately terrified by the thought that I *wouldn't* finish it, and then terrified by the thought that I *would* finish it. How unnerving to realize that *real* people— friends and strangers alike—will actually read these words.

Will my words be helpful? Will they minister? Will they accomplish the desired goal?

Time and time again, I have admitted to the Lord, "I'm terrified. I can't concentrate. I'm afraid that I will disappoint You, that I will fail to carry out the task that You have given me. I feel so weak, so inadequate." And then I quiet myself and listen for His inaudible answer.

It always goes something like this: "Relax. Get back to work. I'm going to help you get this done—you don't have to worry. Do your best, trust My guidance, and leave the rest to Me. Go out from this quiet moment refreshed and strengthened, for I have not given you 'a spirit of timidity, but of power and love and discipline' " (2 Tim. 1:7).

For years I thought of myself as a weak person, and in the flesh I am. I lack the drive, the aggressiveness, and the stability that characterizes stronger personalities. But I have finally realized that my fleshly weakness is really a benefit for me, because it regularly forces me back into the presence of the God of all strength, where I can offer my gift of worship and receive His gift of true power—the power that finds its source not in the limits of human personality, but in the boundless expanse of divine omnipotence.

Powerlessness, fear, timidity. These are words I hate to hear, and feelings I hate to experience. What about you? Do you too feel inadequate and unprepared "to meet the present hour"? If so, turn to the Lord. Worship Him. Remember, He specializes in giving strength to weak people.

Whom Should I Please?

The third problem that I have struggled with is the tendency to listen to too many voices. I don't deny that I am, at heart, a people-pleaser. I want to be everything everybody wants me to be—all the time. If society calls for a superwoman, I want to be one. If my husband calls for a superwife, I want to be one. If my kids call for a supermom, I want to be one. If my church calls for a super-Christian, I want to be one. I want to keep everybody happy. I want to be impressive!

The problem is, of course, that I can't do it. I don't have what it takes to juggle the responsibilities of the 20th-century superwoman-wife-mom-Christian. But still I try. I establish expectations for myself that no one could meet, and then chastise myself because I don't meet them. It's a cruel and vicious cycle.

All my life I've heard people say, "Just be yourself. Don't try to be like anybody else. Find out what *you* do well, and do it." I knew there was truth in those words, but for some reason the truth never passed from theory into practicality. They *sounded* good, but they never touched my real, day-to-day life. I wanted to "be myself"—but it didn't seem that I could be myself and still please everybody else. So I clung to my unrealistic expectations and went on my "people-pleasing" way.

But a strange and life-changing thing happened this year. Worship has a way of making us vulnerable and open. In worship, I found myself saying things like, "Lord, I want to please You. I want to serve You. I want to use what You have given me to help others. But I can't seem to do it. I can't keep up the pace. I feel torn and frustrated and exhausted. I'm trying to please *everybody,* and I'm pleasing no one. I'm trying to do everything, and I seem to accomplish nothing."

Like David, I began to express my feelings and my frustrations, and as God responded to him, so He began to respond to me.

"Just be yourself," He said. "Don't try to be like anybody else. Find out what you do well, and do it. I made you as you are for a purpose. Be yourself." There they were again—those same old words. But this time there was a difference—an addition. "I made you. . . ." These were the words of my Creator, the One I ultimately had to please.

Do you know what it's like to have your Creator tell you that you don't have to live up to all your unrealistic expectations in order to please Him? That you don't have to be all things to all people? That you don't have to listen to all the voices? It's wonderful! It's an unspeakable relief!

It was as if God said to me, "Lynne Hybels, I have something very important to tell you. You are living a life I never intended for you. You're assuming responsibilities I never designed for you. You're trying to please people who have no idea what your abilities and interests are. *I* created you. *I* know what you can do. *I* know what you enjoy. And *I* know best how you can serve Me and other people. Why don't you listen to *Me?*"

He continued, "About this superwoman business, forget it! You don't need an impressive career to be a somebody. You don't need a list of flashy accomplishments to be worthwhile. I didn't create you to be an organizer or an administrator. I never intended for you to jump on the bandwagon of community involvement. So don't worry about those things. I created other people with higher energy levels and stronger leadership abilities to handle those responsibilities.

"And what about this superwife ideal? Be honest. Did your husband ever ask you to be superwife? Did he ever ask you to be a gourmet cook, or an interior decorator, or a great entertainer? Of course not! He only asks that you love him and do your best to meet his legitimate needs. The rest of these burdensome superwife demands are nothing more than your feeble attempts to portray an impressive image. Forget about that and focus on loving your husband.

"And as far as your kids are concerned, they've never even heard of a supermom. They just want someone to love them, and spend time with them, and make them feel special. You feel guilty because you haven't enrolled them in every class from gymnastics to candle-making, you don't serve them homemade apple pies for after-school snacks, and you haven't read the Children's Bible to them from cover to cover. Don't you know that there's more than one way to be a good mother? Only you know the unique needs of your family, and only you are equipped to meet them.

"And now we come to the super-Christian issue. Lynne, there are no super-Christians. There are only regular Christians who decide to be obedient to Me. That's all I ask. That's the essence of the successful Christian life. Just listen to what I say and then do it!

"And one more thing," He continued, "I have given some people in My church numerous gifts because I want them to accomplish a variety of goals. I have given other people only one gift because I want them to concentrate on a given task with their undivided attention. I know best how I can use each person.

"So, if I give you one gift, don't try to serve Me in the same way as the person who has two gifts—and if I give you two gifts, don't think you are any less valuable than the person with four gifts. Just be faithful. I have given you everything you need to live a life that pleases Me.

"Now, relax and live with joy. And whenever you start to get confused, focus your attention on Me, and you'll be at peace."

I claim no hot line to heaven. In fact, it has taken me years to learn to quiet my heart enough to "hear" the inaudible words of God. Even now I feel that I am a beginner, a novice listener. I am sure there is much more that God could communicate to me if I were more adept at hearing His still small voice.

What about you? Have you taken the time to listen to God? Are you aware that He is anxious to communicate to you? That He has words you desperately need to hear?

When you finish this chapter, why not put this book down, and *worship Him*? As you focus your attention on the living God, and exalt Him with your attitude and your words, you will experience His presence in a new way. And as you develop a disciplined worship pattern, you may be surprised to notice a gradual change in your perspective—a change that will positively affect every area of your life.

12
My Life— A Living Sacrifice

Don't forget to bring a sharp carving knife. Everyone must have a knife!

Quickly I read the memo which my husband had sent to all those attending the Labor Day Retreat. Most of the information contained therein was routine. It was just what I had expected. Only those two short sentences at the bottom of the page hinted at an element of mystery. I knew most of the plans for the weekend and I couldn't figure out why we all needed knives.

Then I remembered. Several days earlier as we discussed the weekend schedule, Bill casually mentioned that there was going to be one activity that he would tell no one about—not even me. Could that have something to do with the required knives? I would find out soon enough.

Approximately 80 of us made the 10-hour bus trip to our camp in upper Michigan. We traveled during the night, arriving early Friday morning, exhausted yet excited. These weekends away always proved to be inspiring and challenging. Friday morning and afternoon were spent in relaxation and fun. Some people napped, some swam, some canoed, some played volleyball, and many enjoyed quiet conversations in the shade of the towering hardwood trees.

In the evening, after a hearty camp meal, the first teaching

143

session began. The subject was worship. As Bill taught, we learned that worship is God's ultimate plan for His creation—a plan that was set into action before the foundation of the world and will be continued throughout eternity. For many of us, it was the first time we had seen clearly God's mandate for worship. With anticipation, we looked forward to the next day when we would learn more about this ultimate priority.

Enticed by the wood-scented air and the bright morning sunshine, we rose early and went about our morning chores. A few brave souls bathed in the icy waters of the Tahquamenon River; but most of us quickly washed our hands and faces at the outdoor pump, then headed for the nearest fire to warm up. After breakfast, we joined together for the second session of the weekend. We learned that worship involves the three-pronged response of reverence, submission, and exaltation. We also learned the purpose of our carving knives.

Immediately after the session, we each began searching the camp for a piece of wood approximately 18 inches long. When we found the pieces that suited us, we then began to carve our names on them. Plain or fancy, big or small—we could carve them anyway we wanted to. Given no clue as to what these wooden nameplates would be used for, we knew only that they had to be completed by Sunday evening, before the last session.

As the day progressed, so did our works of art. Some looked like they had been carved by kindergartners, while others were obviously the works of true craftsmen. There was much good-natured sharing, as some of our "sharp" knives proved to be amazingly dull. Unfortunately, there were also a few minor cuts and scratches, for most of us were not too adept at handling such "dangerous" tools.

Throughout the weekend we continued to learn about worship, studying much of the material that was presented in the early chapters of this book.

After the last session on Sunday night, we enjoyed a time of personal sharing. Volunteers stood before the group and explained what the weekend had meant to them, or how it had affected their outlook on worship, or how they would change as a result of their new understanding of God's plan for them. Many people read psalms and prayers they had written in their new worship journals, and others read Scripture passages that called them to worship.

Without a doubt, it was the highlight of the weekend. Even after the last person had spoken, we remained seated, silently enjoying the aura of sanctity which draped the rustic room. It had been a hallowed evening. As individuals and as a unit we had worshiped God, and in our worship we had become overwhelmingly aware of His presence.

Finally, Bill broke the silence by explaining the purpose of the carvings we had created and brought with us that evening. In response to his explanation, we walked slowly outside and stood around a huge bonfire that had been started in a clearing not far from the lodge. As we watched, the flames propelled bright sparks into the night sky and sent slender streams of smoke sailing beyond the highest branches and slithering unseen into the vast darkness.

For a few moments we just waited, reverently, yet expectantly. The heat of the fire warmed us, and the elf-like shadows danced on our faces. Then, one by one we walked slowly toward the huge fire, and when we got as close as the intense heat would allow, we carefully laid our personalized carvings in the midst of the flame. As we watched, the blue tongues licked playfully at the letters that formed our names, then ruthlessly devoured them. Again, we watched the smoke drift slowly out of sight.

In those quiet, meditative moments we knew that it was more than wooden carvings that we were throwing on the all-consuming fire. In that symbolic gesture, we were laying our lives on the altar of sacrifice, as a conscious act of worship.

The Soothing Aroma

In Exodus 29 we read some interesting instructions regarding the worship practices of the Israelites. "And you shall offer up in *smoke* the whole ram on the altar; it is a burnt offering to the Lord; it is a *soothing aroma,* an offering by fire to the Lord" (v. 18).

Later we read about another type of offering, the wave offering. "And you shall take them from their hands, and offer them up in *smoke* on the altar on the burnt offering for a *soothing aroma* before the Lord; it is an offering by fire to the Lord" (v. 25).

About another offering we read, "And the other lamb you shall offer at twilight, and shall offer as the grain offering of the morning with its libation, for a *soothing aroma,* an offering by fire to the Lord. It shall be a *continual burnt offering throughout your generations* at the doorway of the tent of meeting before the Lord, where I will meet with you, to speak to you there" (vv. 41-42).

Then God instituted yet another form of worship, the altar of burnt incense. "And Aaron shall burn *fragrant incense* on it; he shall burn it *every morning* when he trims the lamps. And when Aaron trims the lamps at twilight, he shall burn *incense.* There shall be *perpetual incense* before the Lord *throughout your generations*" (30:7-8).

The primary significance of the sacrificial system ordained in the Old Testament was that it was predictive of the redemptive work that Jesus would accomplish at Calvary. There is, however, another secondary significance to the burnt offerings. God was not just concerned about the animal that was slain and sacrificed. Also important to Him was the fragrance, the soothing aroma. God wanted this pleasing aroma to be drifting upward continually, perpetually, all the time, throughout all generations—as a symbol of worship.

It was as if He were saying, "It is My desire that there be an unending flow of worship rising heavenward, forever. Each time you walk by the doorway of the tent of meeting, you will see the smoke rising from the altar and remember that you ought to be living in a perpetual state of worship. From your heart there ought to be a fragrant aroma of worship rising heavenward at all times."

That is the secondary significance of the sacrificial system. It was a visual teaching aid used by God to impress upon the Israelites the importance of continual worship.

The New Testament affirms this Old Testament truth. "I urge

you therefore, brethren, by the mercies of God, to present your bodies a living and holy sacrifice, acceptable to God, which is your spiritual service of worship" (Rom. 12:1). Day and night, the soothing aroma of the burnt offerings ascended to the throne of heaven as a symbol of adoration and worship. But it was just that—only a symbol. In reality, it is not the fragrant aroma of perfumed incense which pleases God, but rather the perpetual, practical sacrifice of lives bathed in the fragrance of true worship.

Paul affirms this truth again when he identifies himself as a "drink offering" (2 Tim. 4:6). Most scholars agree that the paragraphs which contained those words were among the last Paul ever wrote.

Imagine the great Apostle Paul, the missionary par excellence, the "point man" of the New Testament church, as he nears the end of his life. As he writes this letter to his beloved Timothy, he thinks back over the last few years and analyzes the meaning of his life as a follower of Jesus. His conclusion? That there is nothing he would rather call himself than an offering—a living sacrifice, a perpetual and pleasing aroma. For the Christian there is no higher call, no greater goal.

What does this insight mean for those of us who desire to be true worshipers of the living God? It means that we have to release our worship from the bounds of Sunday morning rituals. We even have to free it from the restraints of our sanctuaries of solitude. In order to become *living* sacrifices, we must make worship a continual part of our lives, a moment by moment gift to God.

Lifestyle Worship

I arrived at this point in this chapter several days ago, but for some reason I could go no further. I knew in essence what I wanted to say, but I just couldn't find the right words. I had to take a break.

Feeling the need to absorb someone else's insights, I decided to read. In the two days that followed, I read two very different books. One was based on the conversations and letters of a humble monk who lived in the 17th century and spent most of his time doing menial labor in a monastery kitchen. The other was authored by a brilliant lawyer of the 20th century whose work has taken him from the inner rooms of the White House to the filthy corners of prison cells.

In *The Practice of the Presence of God,* based on the insights of Brother Lawrence, I was challenged to worship God continually through the avenue of my thought life. In *Loving God,* a book by Charles Colson of Watergate fame and founder of Prison Fellowship, I was challenged to worship God continually through the avenue of my actions.

Thoughts and actions. Basically they are the substance of life. Obviously, if we learn to worship God through them, we will become true lifestyle worshipers. But where do we begin?

In Thought—The Worship of Adoration

Very little is known of the man called Brother Lawrence who has so profoundly affected generations of Christians in the three centuries since he lived. Uneducated and lowly, he served as a lay brother among the barefooted Carmelites in Paris in the latter part of the 17th century. He died at the age of 80, having lived a life ablaze with the joy of knowing God. The record of his conversations and letters is filled with the testimony of one who had learned that the key to walking with God was worship. To adore and exalt God was his unquestioned goal in life.

"Do not, then, forget Him," he wrote, "but think on Him often, adore Him continually, live and die with Him; this is the glorious employment of a Christian. In a word, this is our profession; if we do not know it, we must learn it. . . . I worshiped Him the oftenest that I could, keeping my mind in His holy presence, and recalling it as often as I found it wandered from Him" (*The Practice of the Presence of God,* Fleming H. Revell Co., pp. 54, 31).

Brother Lawrence was not one for theological debate or doctrinal discussion. He wanted to know God, and he pursued the simplest and most direct route to that goal. He decided to live with a constant and practical awareness of God's presence. He determined to think of God continually, converse with Him regularly, and express his love for Him in every way he could.

"We must know before we can love," he wrote. "In order to know God, we must often think of Him; and when we come to love Him, we shall also think of Him often, for our heart will be with our treasure" (p. 53). In thinking of God often, Brother Lawrence learned what godly men and women before and after him have also learned. That God reveals Himself to those who worship Him. That He gives an awareness of His presence to those who seek Him earnestly. And that He responds to the faith of His children with unmatched and unmerited blessing.

In obedience to the regulations of his monastic order, Brother Lawrence maintained the set schedule of private prayers, but he refused to relegate his communion with God to those few isolated moments. "The time of business does not with me differ from the time of prayer; and in the noise and clatter of my kitchen, while several persons are at the same time calling for different things, I possess God in as great tranquility as if I were upon my knees at the blessed sacrament" (p. 29). Conversing with God was the norm—not the exception—in his life, and it was that norm to which he attributed all the richness and reality of his Christian life.

Through the avenue of our thought life, we can turn any moment into a hallowed one. We can transform any time or place or situation into an altar of sacrifice by offering God the fragrant aroma of silent worship.

"He requires no great matters of us: a little remembrance of Him from time to time; a little adoration; sometimes to pray for His grace, sometimes to offer Him your sufferings, and sometimes to return Him thanks for the favors He has given you. . . . The least little remembrance will always be acceptable to Him. You need not cry very loud; He is nearer to us than we are aware of" (p. 48).

I have read Brother Lawrence's little book many times, but since my last reading of it I have tried to apply the truths contained therein with even greater diligence. I have consciously tried to think of God often, and have made it a point to offer Him my "little adorations." What have I learned through this effort?

First, that there is no greater merit in any other activity of our minds. A mere thought in God's direction, a quick word of thanksgiving, a silent sense of awe, can so change the attitude of my heart and mind that I really become a new person. What brings about the change? A silent remembrance of God which leads me to submission and humility. How the quality of our lives would change if we lived in constant awareness of God's love and wisdom and power and majesty!

Second, I have learned how easily I am distracted. In this most worthy art of worship, I remain a novice. I am a beginner. My thoughts still flow too readily from the Lord and back onto myself. It is still too easy for me to make *myself* the object of my devotion, the center of my thoughts.

So what do I do? I retreat to my place of solitude. There I center my thoughts once again on the majestic and glorious God, I confess to Him my self-centeredness, I humbly beg His forgiveness, then I bask in the warmth of His love and forgiveness, and offer once again my gift of worship.

For most of us, sinful as we are, worship must begin as a discipline. But as we practice it faithfully, we find that somewhere along the way it has become less of a discipline and more of a spontaneous response to what we know of God.

"That the end we ought to propose to ourselves is to become, in this life, the most perfect worshipers of God we can possibly be, as we hope to be through all eternity" (Brother Lawrence, p. 25).

For Brother Lawrence, worshiping in adoration and silent exaltation became a way of life. He knew fully the joy of spontaneous response to God. And me? Well, I am still a beginner. But I am making progress, taking feeble steps from the discipline of solitude to the spontaneity of continual thought-life worship. And with each tiny step, I reach a new level of joy and a deeper awareness of the nearness of God.

In Action—The Worship of Obedience

It did not surprise me that one who honored God so beautifully with his thought life would also recognize the importance of honoring Him with his actions. In his writing, Brother Lawrence made it clear that "it was a great delusion to think that the times of prayer ought to differ from other times; that we are as strictly obliged to adhere to God by action in the time of action as by prayer in the season of prayer" (p. 24). It is, in fact, most natural and expected that worship in thought—if it is sincere—will automatically lead us to worship in action.

This was also the premise of Charles Colson's book: that our love for God ought not be merely an indescribable feeling or a thoughtless mouthing of empty words. It ought to be translated into practical terms. In a discussion with His disciples, Jesus said, "If you love Me, you will keep My commandments" (John 14:15). In that statement He set down the inevitable expression of true love and worship; plain, old-fashioned obedience.

Colson wrote *Loving God* because he detected in many Christians a lack of understanding of what it means to love God. When he asked Christians how they showed their love for God, he was met with oft-used clichés that held little tangible meaning, or with open frustration (*Loving God,* Zondervan, p. 15). His book, which is beautifully written, makes it clear that if we want to love God, we must know His Word and apply it to our lives—no matter how difficult or inconvenient that may be. If we want to be true worshipers, loving God in action as well as in thought, we must learn to obey.

In His Word, God tells us the same thing. He relates worship to obedience. For example, in Romans 14, a chapter devoted to instructing people how to get along better with one another, we read, "For he who in this way serves Christ is acceptable to God and approved by men" (v. 18). That little phrase *acceptable to God* is the same phrase which is connected with an appropriate offering of worship. And to what does it refer in this passage? To "the things which make for peace and the building up of one another" (v. 19).

Paul is telling us that if we relate to one another in a way that is consistent with the directives given in God's Word, our relationships can be expressions of acceptable worship.

Imagine that! With every encounter, we have the opportunity to worship God. Every time we come face-to-face with another human being, we have the opportunity to send a sweet-smelling fragrance into the presence of God.

Or we can send the stench of sin. Like Cain, we can present an unacceptable offering. Like the Israelites chastened by the Prophet Malachi, we can present a blemished lamb. In our relationships we can dishonor God and contaminate the offering of our lives.

That truth hit me like a slap in the face—and it continues to do so. I cannot worship God with sincerity in the protected privacy of my office, and then dishonor God in my relationships with my husband and kids. It's great for me to worship God in solitude and in my thought life, but I *must* take that attitude of humble submission and willing obedience into my relationships. I must behave in my relationships the way God tells me to in His Word.

Bill and I have been married for 10 years. Because of the differences in our personalities, our socio-economic backgrounds, our family structures, etc., we came to marriage with some very different expectations; and we have had to work hard to bring those expectations into conformity and establish a peace-filled marriage. Fortunately, we were both willing to work, and we have seen constant progress; but never have we experienced the amount of progress and the level of compatibility that we have enjoyed during the past year. To what do we attribute this growth? To our mutual desire to be more pleasing worshipers.

We want our marriage to be an acceptable offering. We want the fragrance of our conversations to be sweet. We want the aroma of our relationship to bring pleasure to the heart of God. As an act of worship we have become closer friends, more loyal companions, and more sensitive lovers. And I believe God has been very pleased with that.

The same must be true in our relationships with our children, our neighbors, our employers or employees, and our co-workers. Do you realize that it might be an act of worship for you to play a game with your daughter, or go sledding with your son, or cook a meal for your neighbor, or write a note to your mother? Through each of these simple activities, you can delight God with the soothing aroma of obedience.

In speaking of his call to take the Gospel to the Gentiles, the

Apostle Paul's desire was "that my offering of the Gentiles might become acceptable, sanctified by the Holy Spirit" (Rom. 15:16). Again we read of an acceptable offering. And where was it to be found? In Paul's ministry of evangelism. Each conversation wherein he testified to the mercy and grace of God was offered as an act of worship. Each individual who responded to his message by humbling himself before God was viewed not as one more notch on Paul's ladder to success, but as one more worshiper who could lift his voice in praise of God.

In Paul's letter to the church at Philippi, he thanked the Philippians for the gracious financial gift they had sent him and commended them for their repeated generosity. Then he said, "But I have received everything in full, and have an abundance; I am amply supplied, having received from Epaphroditus what you have sent, a fragrant aroma, an acceptable sacrifice, well-pleasing to God" (Phil. 4:18). In this passage Paul reveals another form of true worship—giving.

Each time we give of the resources with which God has blessed us, we have the opportunity to worship Him. When we place our tithe in the offering plate, when we give a special gift above and beyond our tithe to support a special ministry, when we give to those in need, when we help the poor, we have the opportunity to say, "Thank you Father for Your generosity to me. With a joyful heart, I offer this gift as an act of worship."

When the offering plate passes down your row next Sunday, you can give grudgingly, resenting what God asks of you; or you can give joyfully, thankful for one more way to tangibly express your love for God. The next time you see a legitimate financial need which you believe God would have you meet, you can either turn away and claim that "you are not your brother's keeper," or you can give of your God-given resources and send a fragrant aroma into the heavens.

Yes, in our relationships we can worship God. In our efforts to share the Good News we can worship God. In our giving—of our time, our talents, and our treasures—we can worship God. But they are only examples. In reality, there is not one tiny particle of our lives that should not be touched by worship of the living

God. Each act of service, each prayer of intercession, each gift of kindness can be an offering of heartfelt worship.

The Joy of Personal Worship

Brother Lawrence said, "There is not in the world a kind of life more sweet and delightful than that of a continual conversation with God. Those only can comprehend it who practice and experience it; yet I do not advise you to do it from that motive. *It is not pleasure which we ought to seek in this exercise; but let us do it from a principle of love, and because God would have us*" (*The Practice of the Presence of God,* p. 45).

No, it is not for pleasure that we worship God. It is not for what we get out of it. It is because God is worthy of worship, and because He asks for it. That is the only pure motivation for worship. If we had nothing to gain from worship, we would still be obliged to do it.

However, the undeniable truth about worship is that in reality we *do* benefit from it—immeasurably so. There is indeed no "kind of life more sweet and delightful."

In speaking of his life of worship, Brother Lawrence said that it "often causes me joys and raptures inwardly, and sometimes also outwardly, so great that I am forced to use means to moderate them and prevent their appearance to others" (p. 36).

I remember reading those words years ago and shaking my head in total disbelief. What did this man mean by "joys and raptures inwardly"? How could life in a monastery kitchen be so filled with pleasure and "ecstasies of the soul"? I couldn't understand. I was unaware of the connection between worship and joy.

But that was because at that time I was a nonworshiper. And as is true for so many things, worship can only be understood by the one who experiences it. And what does such a one find? That in worship there is joy.

Why? Because worship ushers us into the presence of God. And as David said, "In Thy presence is fulness of joy; in Thy right hand there are pleasures forever" (Ps. 16:11).

There are many things about Christianity that I don't fully understand. There are many matters of the faith that remain a mystery to me. This certainly is one of them. How the conscious activity of focusing our attention upon Another can bring joy to our souls, I do not know. But it happens. And though I am yet a novice worshiper, I have had enough tastes of joy to know beyond doubt that the way of worship is, in fact, the way of joy.

For years, one of my favorite books has been *Surprised by Joy* by C.S. Lewis. As a matter of fact, it will probably be the first book I will read after this manuscript is completed—for I am anxious to once again turn the well-worn pages. But even without lifting its cover, even without reading its first word, I am touched by it. For when I look at the title, I realize that those few words capture the "bonus" of my worship experience. In the past year, I have been repeatedly, "surprised by joy." In offering God my gift of worship, I have received the invaluable gift of joy—a gift undeserved and unexpected, but appreciated beyond words.

For all practical purposes, life is made up of a series of decisions. Each minute, we decide how we will think, how we will act, how we will respond; and with each of these decisions we have the same choice to make. Will we send to God the fragrant aroma of worship—the sweet smell of adoration and obedience? Or will we defile the heavens with the stench of sin?

The choice is mine. And yours.